THE ORGANISATION AND MANAGEMENT OF EDUCATIONAL TECHNOLOGY

NEW PATTERNS OF LEARNING SERIES
Edited by P.J. Hills, University of Surrey

AN INTRODUCTION TO EDUCATIONAL COMPUTING
Nicholas John Rushby

PREPARING EDUCATIONAL MATERIALS
N.D.C. Harris

THE ORGANISATION AND MANAGEMENT OF EDUCATIONAL TECHNOLOGY
Richard N. Tucker

The Organisation and Management of Educational Technology

RICHARD N. TUCKER

CROOM HELM LONDON

Croom Helm Ltd, 2-10 St John's Road, London SW11

British Library Cataloguing in Publication Data

Tucker, Richard N
The organisation and management of educational technology. - (New patterns of learning series).
1. Educational technology
I. Title II. Series
371.3'078 LB1028.3

ISBN 0-85664-941-4

Printed in Great Britain by
Biddles Ltd, Guildford, Surrey

CONTENTS

Acknowledgements

Prologue

Introduction 9
The Institutions 9

1. The Problem of Definitions 11
A Parable 13

2. The Institutions 15
Colleges of Further Education 15; The Colleges of Education 20; Colleges of Higher Education/Polytechnics 22; Universities 25

3. What Is to Be Serviced 28
Learn to Listen 30; Don't Assume Any Subject Knowledge 31; Learn to Ask Questions 31; Find Out What Is Required 32; Find Out What Exists Already 33; If the Parts of an Answer Exist, Bring Them Together 34; Create the Resources 34

4. Information 39
Information and the Librarian 42; Information on Hardware Purchase 47; Information on Software Held within the Institution 50; Information on Hardware Held within the Institution 54; Information about Incoming Materials 62; Evaluative Data 64; Inter-Institutional Information 67; Information Networks outside the Institution 68

5. Organisation of Support Services 73
The Organisation of Software 74; The Organisation of Hardware 89; Development of the Resource Centre and Resource Organisation 102; Control of Production and Reproduction 109

6. Strategies for Ensuring the Acceptance of the Educational Technology Services 126
Assimilation 130; Dissemination 132; Staffing and Staff Organisation 135

7. Educational Development 140

8. Summary 145

Bibliography 146
Glossary 156
Appendix 159
Index 165

NEW PATTERNS OF LEARNING

The Purpose of this Series

This series of books is intended to provide readable introductions to trends and areas of current thinking in education. Each book will be of interest to all educators, trainers and administrators responsible for the implementation of educational policies and programmes in higher, further and continuing education.

The books are designed for ease of access of information. Each contains a glossary of important terms in the subject and has an annotated bibliography of key works to enable the reader to pursue selected areas in depth should he or she so wish.

This book, *The Organisation and Management of Educational Technology*, examines the service and support roles in which the educational technologist is the human filter for the needs of both staff and students. Techniques for analysing requests and assisting the enquirer towards appropriate solutions are outlined. The book is written by Richard Tucker who is a Senior Assistant Director of the Scottish Council for Educational Technology.

P.J. Hills.
Guildford, 1979.

ACKNOWLEDGEMENTS

No book which attempts to describe an existing set of circumstances and dares to draw conclusions from observations can be the work of any one person. My own experience of twelve years work in educational technology has furnished only a small part of what appears in these pages. So much has come from the ideas, experience and judgements of others that it is impossible to thank them all individually for the help and guidance that they have given to me.

Many of the ideas have been distilled from a series of interviews conducted with people who are carrying out the daily task of administering educational technology support services in a wide range of educational establishments. To those who gave so freely of their time and were so frank in their answers, I extend my heartfelt thanks. I hope that they can recognise the points they made and that no reader can identify them or their institutions. Thanks must also go to all those people who through word or practice have shaped the structure of this book unknowingly, especially those colleagues in Scotland with whom one has the privilege of working from time to time.

I am particularly grateful to Alex Logan, Dr Philippe Duchastel and Richard Hooper for their kind permission to use their work, to my colleagues at the Scottish Council for Educational Technology who have helped in so many ways, to Dr Philip Hills for his patient and gentle guidance as editor and to Moira Goodall and Ann Franchi for being able to transcribe my handwriting.

PROLOGUE

Once upon a time there was an old lady who lived in a house. She had a husband and children and she was contented with her lot. She did everything for her family she could. She washed and scrubbed all their clothes and her husband's shirts and children's blouses were whiter than white. She polished and shone the house till her arms ached, and, because it was for her family, she did not mind. Every now and then she would dip into her cook book and make something tasty for tea. Every night she retired late, never managing to have time to watch the 'telly' with her family. She was contented however. She knew she was doing her best.

Sometimes vacuum cleaner salesmen, washing machine salesmen, carpet shampoo salesmen, would call but she never had time to listen to them. She was busy attending to her family. She did notice occasionally, when she paused at the sink, other women out walking with their families and talking to each other animatedly. She stifled her curiosity, as to how they managed the time, with the thought that their homes must be neglected and returned with dedicated vigour to her chores.

Then one day she slid on a wet floor and died. Her family mourned her briefly — but they had not known her well. They used the insurance money to buy a cooker with a timing device, a fully automated washing machine, stretch covers for the three piece suite and talked animatedly to each other between programmes on the 'telly'.

The moral — it pays to look where you are going.

A. Logan (1972)
after the style of Mager (1962, Pix)

INTRODUCTION

Discussion of organisation and management usually opens with a statement of the subject content, the place and the people. In the case of educational technology we are dealing with something which is not in itself a 'subject' in an academic sense and is only now beginning to receive institutional recognition through the establishment of courses.

As many writers have already made clear, there is no single definition of educational technology. For those who work in the field it is what they do, and for the daily round no clearer definition is sought. When the 'educational technologist' is asked to define his subject he tends to seek the cover of the broad definitions that encompass the whole range of educational technology activities, from the analytical methods of the educational psychologist to the audio-visual technician and store keeper. But the way in which one sees educational technology rather depends on where one stands within the educational spectrum.

For the purpose of this book we must deal with all the constituent parts of educational technology. The building of evaluation techniques into the construction of new curricular materials is essential to the effective organisation and development of the teaching and learning process, but is not always seen as something that has implications for the person with day-to-day responsibility for educational technology. Here educational technology plays an effective role in the systematic development of education. It is not the place of this book to discuss those techniques themselves but to indicate the role that they can have within the organisation and management of educational technology in an institution.

Therefore we must consider the systems approach to education in the light of the implications, for those that have to organise and manage, that follow on from the selection of various methodologies, materials and modes of evaluation and assessment. The suggestions that will be put forward are essentially pragmatic, being based on the experiences of those who have been charged with the organisation and management of educational technology in a wide range of post-school institutions.

The Institutions

In the context of this book educational technology will be considered within its institutional setting, for whilst there are matters of organisation and management that affect each individual teacher these are dependent upon the patterns of organisation and support determined by the institution.

When one considers the post-compulsory education field there are obviously many types of establishment. But while they have numerous elements in common, which must be recognised as a basic core around which to build organisational patterns, there are also a great many differences between establishments. For the purpose of this book we shall be considering institutions as widely different as the small college of further education and the large polytechnics and the universities.

Differences arise from the people that work within the various institutions as much as from the physical differences of size, and we will be returning to the human factor many times throughout the book.

1 THE PROBLEM OF DEFINITIONS

What is meant by educational technology in the context of organisation and management? The broad definitions* refer to systematic approaches to the problems of teaching and learning. From the start it should be recognised that, whilst it is possible to consider the practical problems of equipment storage, bibliographic control of data or the production of learning materials without reference to the educational context, this can only be a short-term view since it will, of necessity, ignore the implications of decisions taken about the curriculum, the chosen methodologies and the desired outcomes.

Most of the attention of this book will be given to the practical solutions and questions arising from the provision of support services to education, but it will be within the context of giving first place within the chain of decisions to the educational needs.

Distinctions have been made between the 'technologies *of* education' and 'technology *in* education' in an attempt to clarify the different aspects of the activities that are frequently grouped together under 'educational technology'. This has been essential in demonstrating that there is a valid place within educational technology for the psychologist and the media producer.

Although the definitions that have been provided for us — those that separate out the methodological, pedagogical and evaluative aspects of education from the supportive aspects such as production, resource organisation and equipment control — have been useful in helping those who have entered educational technology to recognise that there are other aspects with equally valid specialisations, it is arguable that we should no longer cling to these definitions. They are now beginning to act as divisive rather than cohesive touch-stones.

The practical implications in the organisation of support services which will be looked at in this book can arise from the provision, within an institution, of a whole range of resources which are not related to the needs of the teachers and learners. That they should spring from the learning needs makes better educational and managerial sense.

In an ideal situation the resource organiser would be starting with a new and empty institution, into which the staff move — having been given time to plan, analyse and synthesise the learning objectives.

* See definitions in Appendix.

Applying a systematic approach to the curriculum, they would then be able to devise courses which would have the inbuilt elements of assessment and evaluation — each of these feeding back to mechanisms which would improve whatever learning materials had been developed. From this would grow a system of organisation of the learning materials and equipment that is required.

We do not live in an ideal world. It is axiomatic that the educational technologist will be working in a situation in which somebody else has already taken a decision which precludes some actions and predetermines others. It is a fair reflection of the contemporaneous nature of the 'technology of education' and 'technology in education'. For a distinct problem one might be able to take a systems approach. Equally we can take a systematic approach to the more general problems. Life however is not systematic, it does not progress with a linear logic. Decisions are taken about courses before those who have to develop them have had a chance to work out aims and objectives. Money has to be planned for in budgets so far ahead that those responsible for selection of equipment cannot be provided with adequate data on which to base those decisions.

If this suggests a picture of chaos in education we should not be shocked or depressed. These are the basic conditions for virtually every walk of life. Education itself has survived and continues to develop. In our ideal world the technologies *of* education come first. A close look will show that many of the theoretical developments in modern thinking arise from the new freedoms provided by mechanised and electronic aids, and in some cases the methodological development has sprung directly from the intrinsic logic of the machine. By the same token some teaching machine systems have been developed in order to solve problems set by pedagogical needs and by the desires of those developing new methodologies.

Just as in the developmental stages it is not always possible to separate the 'of' and 'in' types of educational technology, so in the institutional setting there are so many factors modifying the practice of education that one cannot easily separate out the elements. Rather than educational technology being of two sorts, it is important that the educator and administrator alike see educational technology as being a spectrum of many things bound together by that aspect of being systematic in approach and content-free.

If one sees educational technology as both a method of leading and developing education and yet at the same time supporting what is being put into practice now, then the notion of a spectrum covers the theoretical developmental aspects (what has been called the 'under-

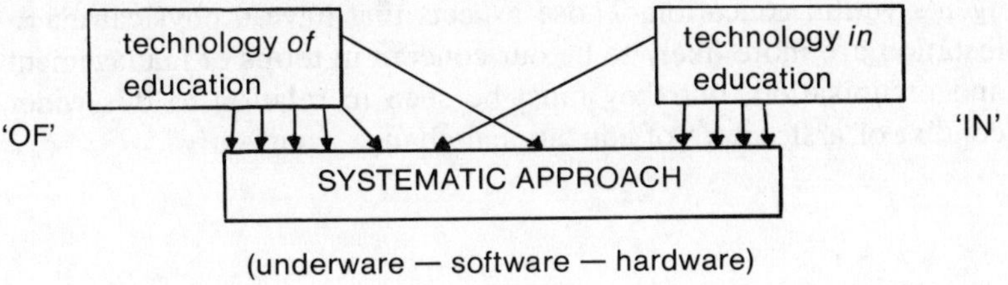

ware', the materials that are produced to enable the teacher and learners to achieve their objectives more readily (the 'software'), and the equipment that is necessary to use, store and retrieve that software (the 'hardware'). All these elements are interdependent within their own system.

The people who operate at various points along that spectrum have not always recognised that they are dependent upon each other. The academic and professional levels may differ, but in isolation their work cannot fully flower. The technician may dismiss or be dismissed by the theoretician, but without each other there would be no system in which to work.

A Parable

The captain of a ship, having been harangued by his chief engineer as being a strutting peacock who did little other than point the ship in the direction of the next port, offered to change places with the engineer to see how he would manage on the bridge.

His bluff having been called, the captain found himself in the engine room faced by a mass of knobs and levers.

After many rings on the engine telegraph, and some wild manoeuvres of the engines resulting from his tentative button-pushing, the captain swallowed his pride and telephoned the chief engineer on the bridge.

'I can't work these blasted engines of yours,' he admitted.

'Don't worry,' came the reply, 'you couldn't use them now in any case. I've just run the ship on to a sandbank.'

Educational technology is all of the things the definitions say; it is also all the things that educational technologists do, but there is one other definition worth considering. If we accept that technologies are methods of operating things or systems of thought which are designed to create change — if they are 'change agents' — then educational technology should encompass a wide range of 'systems' both intellectual and physical, which individually and collectively act as change agents within education. Those aspects that have a physical manifestation are more likely to be our concern in terms of management and organisation, but they must be seen in relation to this wider context of a structure of educational change agents.

2 THE INSTITUTIONS

The literature on the organisation of educational technology has tended to concentrate on the experience of the large institutions. The larger the teaching staff, the easier it is to argue the need for a separate unit to service the educational technology needs of the institution. It is therefore not surprising that the best-known examples of educational technology organisation have come from universities, polytechnics and colleges of education.

The literature has also tended to focus on the topic in a fairly narrow way; support services provided by 'the audio-visual aids department', 'television services' and the 'educational development unit', etc. These practical aspects of support service organisation will be covered in later chapters where they will be set in the broad context of educational technology.

Firstly, however, we shall examine the institutional setting of organisational technology.

Colleges of Further Education

These are the most numerous of all the institutions we will be considering. Almost every town of any size has a college of further education. The larger towns and cities can usually boast a range of colleges.

The majority of colleges of further education share a background in vocational education. Thus, whilst most of the colleges will offer the opportunity for further study towards the examinations that can be taken at school, one tends to find major concentrations of vocational courses related to the industries of that particular region. For example, areas such as South Yorkshire or South Wales have colleges offering courses in subjects relating to coal mining. Equally, one finds colleges in most areas that offer courses in secretarial and clerical skills, hairdressing and catering. Courses related to essential service jobs such as plumbing, electrical engineering and building can be found spread across the country.

Amongst these colleges of further education one finds examples of colleges which were established to cater for specific subjects when there was a sufficiently large demand — subjects such as domestic science, food technology, building, printing, commercial subjects. Naturally these more specialised institutions are usually found in the larger conurbations where the size of the local population can support the numbers required to run the courses. Few of these more specialised colleges have remained single-discipline institutions. A natural development of other subject departments has taken place so that one finds a small number of other subjects being taught, more or less related to the main concern of the college. As a result many of these colleges are divided into a fairly small number of departments and are in this respect not unlike the normal college of further education. Whilst this is admittedly an over-simplification, it does highlight some factors that are important in considering the organisation of educational technology within them.

Vocational training has been, and rightly remains, the main function of such colleges. Because the courses are related to the needs of the industries or professions that they serve there are well established and successful methods used within these courses.

It follows naturally under these circumstances that most of the transmission of knowledge is in the mode of 'training' rather than 'teaching'. Whilst recognising that many changes are taking place, 'training' still remains the dominant 'mode'. This in no way downgrades the function of 'training', for it has long since been proved to be the most successful mode of learning for the needs of the colleges and the students.

Where 'teaching' in the more traditionally accepted form of the 'transmitter – receiver' relationship of teacher and student is to be found, it is either as an adjunct to the main core of job training or within the departments catering for those students taking 'school' examinations. It is unfortunate that such departments are undeniably regarded as a less important function of the college by many members of staff.

Because of the concentration on training there has been a tradition within the colleges for appointing staff who were themselves qualified and experienced in a particular skill, rather than selecting staff who had teaching skills as their major qualification.

The skilled craftsman has passed on his skills to the apprentice for centuries, and although courses were devised which formalised this transmission of skills by identifying the component parts and placing them within a linear structure, there was no essential difference between the college course and the old-fashioned apprenticeship. Changes occurred as more and more formal and theoretical elements were added to the basic requirements for qualification. The teams of trainers were joined by teachers of the theoretical elements — subjects such as physics, maths, electronics, etc.

Today there is a balance between the practical and theoretical in the teaching, but there is still a sense among many teaching staff that the 'training' is paramount. Add to this the fact that until recently there was little training given to the trainers in pedagogical methods and one has a situation in which a large number of the staff members, who may be excellent at doing their own job, have never had to concern themselves deeply with the apparently abstract aspects of 'education'.

And why should they? The methods that they employ are well tried, and if any suggestion is to be made that they should change them then an extremely convincing case must be made. The learning materials that they use obviously do the job required of them and there must be good reasons given in suggesting that the teachers add new materials to their resources.

Because of this pattern of work within the colleges and because of the relatively small proportion of staff who have received a modern pedagogical training, there is a natural resistance to change. It is arguable that this traditional stance is a virtue with regard to educational technology, for there is unlikely to be a wholesale acceptance of changes simply because they introduce methods or materials that are 'new'. Any changes that are accepted are likely to have been well scrutinised and adopted slowly and carefully.

The size of a college may have much to do with the rate at which change is assimilated. If there are only a few departments within a college then it appears that they can each be very strong in maintaining their separate identity. As will be seen later, many of the strengths of support organisation rely upon the shared concern of all the departments within an institution and upon a high degree of centralised organisation. In a situation in which departments feel secure and self-sufficient the job of the educational technology organiser is made much harder.

A second function of size that affects the organisation of resources within an institution and therefore affects the whole educational technology approach is that it is very difficult for the small institution to argue the case for adequate staffing for an educational technology unit (no matter what title it is given, or what its remit). Depending on the job description of such a unit there are minimum staffing levels below which the operation cannot be maintained with efficiency, yet few colleges have been able to meet these staffing levels. Indeed many colleges have not yet felt it necessary even to consider the question of staffing the educational technology support. For instance, many colleges have implemented plans for audio-visual support yet this is

Job	Not Done	Done	Teaching Services Officer Educational Technology Unit Educational Technologist Head of Learning Resources Centre	Dept	Dep. Princ ipal	Princ ipal	Libra rian	Tech nician	Ed. Tech. Comm ittee
1. To co-ordinate the acquisition of audio-visual equipment.	2	25	19	-	3	1	-	-	1
2. To co-ordinate the use of audio-visual equipment within the college.	3	24	19	-	1	-	-	2	1
3. To administer a maintenance service for audio-visual equipment located throughout the college.	2	25	18	-	2	1	-	2	1
4. To arrange the instruction of staff in the handling of audio-visual equipment.	3	24	19	-	1	-	-	2	1
5. To organise the recording of radio and TV programmes off air.	3	24	17	1	1	-	-	4	-
6. To organise the replay of recorded TV programmes.	4	23	16	1	-	-	-	5	-
7. To co-ordinate the ordering and distribution of TV and radio support leaflets.	4	23	18	1	1	-	1	-	1
8. To co-ordinate the hiring, distribution and return of films.	4	23	13	5	1	-	3	-	-
9. To inform staff of the recordings and films available in the college during the year.	4	23	16	1	1	-	3	1	-
10. To co-ordinate all book and non-book resources.	15	12	6	-	-	-	6	-	-
11. To maintain with the librarian a									

central bank of information relating to non-book resources.	11	16	7	-	-	-	6	2	-
12. To disseminate information on teaching resources to all lecturing staff.	6	21	17	-	2	-	-	-	1
13. To be responsible for staff development programmes.	13	14	7	-	5	1	-	-	1
14. To advise staff on methods of use of non-book and audio-visual resources and on their effectiveness.	9	18	15	1	-	-	-	-	1
15. To advise students on the use of audio-visual resources.	15	12	10	1	-	-	-	-	-
16. To give professional assistance to college academic staff and to assist in improving their effectiveness.	9	18	13	2	-	-	-	-	2
17. To evaluate student-based programmes and self-teaching techniques within the college.	20	7	5	2	-	-	-	-	-
18. To organise systematic evaluation of teaching methods in college departments.	23	4	1	2	1	-	-	-	-
19. To advise on methods of assessment and of curriculum development in the college.	17	10	5	4	1	-	-	-	-
20. To act as a link between the Scottish Council for Educational Technology and the college.	8	19	17	-	1	-	-	-	-

often the responsibility of a single member of staff. In some cases this is only a part-time function.

The context that has been described above is a broad generalisation but it is one into which the educational technologist is sometimes thrust — or alternatively it is the context from which someone is drawn and has the role of educational technologist thrust upon them.

The existence of someone, or a team, within a specifically supportive role in these circumstances can be seen by some members of staff as a challenge. It may imply a deficiency in what they themselves use as teaching or learning materials. Here the support service has the difficult job of persuasion, requiring the greatest possible tact. If the support service has a defined role which, in the broader sense of educational technology, includes an element of in-service training and staff development, then this must be approached with sensitivity and an appreciation of the great value of the role of the trainer.

The table above shows returns from 27 colleges of further education and illustrates the range of jobs that are expected within the colleges and the persons who execute these functions.

The Colleges of Education

In physical terms colleges of education range from the very small (and rapidly disappearing) to those of a size that rival the small universities. Although they have many subject departments within them the perception of the institution by those within it tends to be more of a cohesive whole, in that ostensibly they have the common purpose of training teachers.

One might expect that within such institutions where 'education' should override any 'subject' division, there would be a natural concern for the methodologies of education and therefore a wide range of learning resources. One would expect to find a natural curiosity about alternative approaches to the teacher-learner relationship.

The degree to which this is so is debatable. Certainly the recognition of the status of audio-visual media within the process of learning to become a teacher is reflected in the fact that virtually all, if not absolutely all, colleges of education have audio-visual units. Built into the student courses are sections on the handling of equipment and the production of audio-visual materials. Such colleges tend to be more concerned about the content and the organisation of the library than many other institutions. This concern may well spring from the desire to inculcate good habits of book use and research techniques.

The question must, however, be raised as to the extent to which the educational technology approach to learning permeates the intellectual fabric of colleges of education. To turn the harsh spotlight of such a question on to the colleges of education may seem to be unfair in contrast to the way in which other institutions tend to be considered. But since educational technology is concerned with both the intellectual and practical tools of education it is only right that the colleges of education should be questioned more severely than any other tertiary institution. It is from these colleges that our teachers come, and if educational technology has any part to play in the improvement of teaching and learning then it must be considered as an essential part of the professional development of teachers. Colleges of education therefore bear a serious responsibility with regard to educational technology.

College audio-visual units usually have the double responsibility of producing materials that are required within the college and at the same time teaching both pre-service and in-service teachers equipment handling and materials production. In all the interviews conducted, colleges visited or articles read, this author has yet to find an audio-visual unit which claims, in its most objective moments, to have adequate staff or time to carry out any one function properly. One only has to look at the small amount of time spent by student teachers during the whole of their training in learning to operate machines and produce materials in order to question the adequacy of what is provided.

It is easy to accuse the colleges of having failed to provide adequate training for the student. It is patently more difficult to propose any practical alternatives. For example, to suggest that more time is devoted to audio-visual aids during training implies that something else goes to the wall. This discussion has centred solely on audio-visual handling and materials production, but the methodological approaches cannot be separated from these.

Methods of teaching and presentation are most clearly considered in all subject departments. It might be suggested that the audio-visual elements of teacher training should not be tucked away in a corner marked 'audio-visual' to be learned for one week per session, but should be an integral part of every department as a natural consequence of a consideration of teaching methods. The implications of this are potentially very expensive, but we will return later in the book to this notion of decentralisation.

A number of points can be made here. Colleges of education *are* creating practical, pragmatic and theoretical developments in the field of educational technology. Courses such as the recently developed Diplomas in Educational Technology are creating interesting changes in the educational model as we know it. The development of colleges themselves has been affected to a large degree by the principles of educational technology — the recent documentation on the development of Dundee College of Education is worthy of careful study.

Yet two facts remain. Most students, having become practising teachers, tend to take up patterns of behaviour which imitate the methods by which they themselves were taught at school and within college. The opportunity to use this mode of learning is not always seized by college staff and raises questions for the use of educational technology within the colleges of education in staff development. There is now evidence in many colleges that students are, for complex reasons, rejecting much of what they receive during a course. It is thought by some that the student in practice then reverts to the model best known, i.e. the school classroom in which they were taught.

The second fact is that a recent survey of teachers' attitudes to resources, their use and organisation (the Resource Liaison Project, conducted by SCET in 1977-9) showed an alarming lack of knowledge and awareness of audio-visual materials and educational technology in general, even amongst recent graduates from a variety of colleges of education, many having fine reputations for their audio-visual and educational technology strengths. This lack of knowledge was accompanied by severe criticism of the colleges themselves for not having trained the teachers to cope with, or use, these modern tools of the profession.

Such criticisms are unjust to any single institution but they appear to carry within them the seeds of a problem. Because of the very nature of what they set out to do, colleges of education are more liable to such criticisms, and they are also easy targets. It must be remembered that the most forceful consideration of these issues comes from within the colleges themselves.

Colleges of Higher Education/Polytechnics

Here one is attempting to describe a wide variety of institutions. A few of these have maintained a physical and organisational structure over a long period, but what characterises most of these institutions is the common factor of growth and change during the last two or three decades.

Technical colleges have expanded, raised the level of their academic awards, and added to the list of departments in response to demand and the changing nature of our technological world. Art colleges join with schools of higher education and catering colleges to be reborn as polytechnics. In shape they may blossom in clear concrete and glass on campus sites, or they may remain as a scatter of older buildings spread across a whole city (or several towns).

Several important aspects of this growth have affected the development of educational technology within these institutions. Firstly the growth took place, or at least began, in a time of economic expansion and in many cases there was a fairly massive input of capital equipment in support of educational technology. This is most apparent in the field of reprography and television. There was a noticeable effect on the attitudes within the institutions. In general people are more ready to accept the sorts of change that are inherent in the educational technology approach during periods of wealth and large-scale resource provision, and there is nothing like money and easy access to resources to help the would-be 'change agent'. As a result there was, at the crucial time, a favourable atmosphere for the establishment of educational technology or educational development units. Those institutions that are currently amalgamating into polytechnics during a period of economic restraint are facing much more serious problems of acceptability of innovation through educational technology.

A further factor which assisted in the assimilation and dissemination was the raising of the academic level of the institutional awards. This served to concentrate attention on the pedagogical skills as well as the subject expertise of staff. Changes in status and attractive pay scales made the polytechnics fierce competitors for the best available teachers.

Whilst there may still be many problems in initiating staff development, circumstances such as those prevailing during the early days of the polytechnics were more favourable than most for such innovation. Thus one can find within polytechnics many examples of extensive and well developed, well equipped educational technology units, providing materials and training in equipment handling, materials production and a whole range of educational methods.

The other end of the spectrum exists, of course; agglomerations of institutions, each at different stages of development, geographically separated, unequally equipped, and with duplications of resource provision, struggling to make some sense of the problem that faces them in their new structure.

Here we see the contrast between the new and custom-built and the agglomerated. Though there may well be excellent examples of good, effective resource management in such institutions the tendencies of human beings militate against success. There is suspicion of new 'units', there is resistance to the enforced relationship; the departmental walls are built a little higher and a little thicker. There is a natural tension resulting from the fear that one of the former component parts will somehow gain ascendency.

It is an extremely difficult job for the directorate of such an institution to replace the former perceptions of the staff members with the concept of a new, simple body. Such changes take time and require the building of individual and institutional confidence, and here the service units, including that which services educational technology, have under these circumstances an important role to play. If they can be seen as being outside all other 'institutional' or 'school' hierarchies in serving only the single institution, and if they can be seen to be providing a reliable and effective service, they can do a great deal to cross boundaries, both real and imaginary.

The major factor in the comparative success of assimilation of educational technology into polytechnics is the 'newness' of the institutions. Staffed by people who are hired for their expertise in a particular subject, these institutions seem to be more ready to accept others with an expertise in providing form for their content. Perhaps because of the newness of the institutions themselves there is a greater readiness to try new methods of teaching and learning, and there appears to be less resistance to the suggestion that what they are doing in their teaching can be improved. Thus in a service role the educational technologist may have a slightly more productive time in a polytechnic than in some other institutions. Though in all the institutions the educational technologist will be asked to provide equipment for this department, a television programme for that department, and a set of slide tape sequences for a third, there does appear to be greater opportunity in some polytechnics to take the discussion with the 'customer' through to the next stage. It is at this point that one begins to explore the implications for the methodology and mode of learning, and it is at this point that the educational technology role begins to change from 'audio-visual supply' to 'staff development'. It is arguable that it is unprofessional simply to supply the 'customer' with his or her audio-visual requirements without making sure that all parties concerned have understood the implications inherent in the choice of a particular medium and have also considered the alternative forms which might have been used. By implications one means not only the need for equipment but also the pedagogical effects that the choice of medium has on teaching method and learning modes, and the whole range of economic implications.

To assume the right to extend the discussion with a client into these areas begins to cause conflicts between the 'audio-visual services' perception of the educational technology role and the 'staff development' or 'educational development' role that is being claimed. This question will be explored later but it appears that at present the most forceful moves in this direction are taking place within the polytechnics of England and Wales and the Central Institutions of Scotland.

Universities

Although going under one title, universities display a diversity as wide as any of the groups so far described. Divided into subject departments within faculties there is a natural element of the territorial imperative, but like the polytechnics and the colleges of further education there is sometimes a willingness to call on the expertise of others so long as it does not impinge upon any subject expertise within the department making the request.

Because of the separation of departments and faculties and the recognition that the universities had what appeared to be special requirements for more developed learning systems, there was, in the 1960s, an examination of the support services required. The Brynmor Jones report (1965) recommended the establishment of television services in selected universities. Such large-scale installations were followed by smaller installations at other universities, such being human nature. Now virtually every university has a television service of some kind, either as part of an audio-visual unit or as a separate entity.

The functions of these units vary but in the main they are designed to provide materials on demand, adding form to other people's content. There are few instances of the media support units being connected in any formal way with those departments which are most likely to be actively concerned with the broader definitions of educational technology. The departments of education and psychology are likely to feel that questions of pedagogical methods, of aims and objectives, of assessment and evaluation are rightly their province. It is not surprising that there is evidence of resistance to moves by 'educational technologists' to lay claim to such aspects of educational development. It is yet another example of the confusion that surrounds the definition and perception of educational technology.

University staff are appointed for their proven excellence in a given subject. This proof is often gained by lonely study yet results in the successful person facing a lecture theatre full of undergraduates. Until the recent moves by the UGC, there was little evidence of staff training in the difficult art of teaching at this advanced academic level, and though undoubtedly there are very many excellent teachers in our universities there might be a case for suggesting that improvements could be made. As will be dealt with later there are problems in carrying out such staff development without damaging self-esteem, but the universities should be fertile ground.

In general, universities are well equipped in terms of materials production. There are perhaps fewer projectors and OHPs to be found than in the secondary school and one can sometimes detect a feeling that using teaching/learning tools instead of the blackboard is somehow intellectually inferior, though of course such aspersions are not cast on useful tools such as laboratory equipment or the omnipresent computer. The distribution of equipment within a university is often affected by the geographical layout, and the separation of faculty buildings militates against the movement of audio-visual equipment and materials. The intellectual separation of the faculties may be an even bigger obstacle to the rationalisation of resources.

Simple stock-taking exercises in several universities have revealed surprising amounts of unknown resources. Each reader must have a horror story or two to match the discovery of an expensive professional 16 mm film camera strapped to a microscope, rarely used and over-sophisticated for the job required — with the university film unit grossly under-equipped; or the large-screen television projector that everybody had forgotten about. One Australian university undertook a stock-taking exercise, instituted by the university accountant as part of a feasibility study for a new centralised resource and educational development unit. The search revealed twenty-one 16 mm cine-cameras. Universities, like all other institutions, should take care to rationalise resource distribution, which does not necessarily mean centralisation or the elimination of all duplication.

The support units that exist within universities have the advantage of working close to colleagues who have a duty to carry out research. Where good relationships have been established between the 'educational technologists' and those in education or psychology departments (who might well regard themselves as educational technologists) then extremely valuable research work has been carried out. It is such fruitful relationships, the examinations of the learning process, that have lead naturally in some instances to changes in the methods of presentation, evaluation and assessment within a department. This is educational development, surely one of the goals of the educational technologist. That such work can be seen most often in universities appears to spring from a relatively wealthy environment which encourages intellectual curiosity and a willingness to be self-critical.

The fact remains, however, that few universities have succeeded in developing coherent resource organisation. There is a great deal of departmental resource development carried out with no consideration of what already exists within the university. It is very difficult for the audio-visual or educational technology unit to intrude into other departments and attempt to advise them on how they should manage their resources, and most departments that have established graphic, photographic and reprographic support will argue strenuously that they make full use of these resources. This is hardly surprising, for it is rare to find an under-used facility where people are concerned — one can often find under-used equipment, but that is another matter — as work tends to expand to use up any available facility.

The question still remains to be asked whether the establishment of such facilities was the most effective course of action in the first place. All too rarely is anyone in a position to co-ordinate the organisation of resources in the university. There is even a sense of irony in some of the cases where there is a unit powerful enough to take a co-ordinating role. Of those universities that were granted the major TV and audio-visual developments, some are now observing an increased resistance to their presence. Although this is not yet clearly articulated one suspects that the very size of the major TV establishments in universities is bringing down on their heads all the lurking fears about monolithic structures, professional interference and so on. It may be that the smaller units, the poorer brethren, have been able to establish better working relationships by having been forced to assume a lower profile.

Whether there is a serious movement of resistance to the large educational technology units remains to be seen but it is an aspect of behaviour that has been observed by more than one unit director. If there is to be any move towards expanding the supportive role of such units into the innovative role of 'educational development' then academic attitudes towards central structures cannot be ignored. This is especially true when a unit which is perceived by outsiders to have a purely 'service' role begins to assume developmental status.

3 WHAT IS TO BE SERVICED

Let us take a pragmatic view of the organisation and management of educational technology. The degree to which the organiser can begin to affect the way that colleagues think and work will depend on many factors, not least of which will be the personalities of those involved. However, it is unlikely that there will be any opportunity to make any effective change if no service is offered. For 'educational technology' to have any place within the institution, for it to be institutionalised, it must first be recognised as the supplier of specified services. If any credibility is then to be maintained that service must be able to fulfil its promises at all times; whatever a service unit claims to be able to do it must actually be able to do. Therefore it is essential in developing any form of resources support unit within an institution that careful consideration should be given to all the implications of early decisions.

There is considerable danger in making grandiose claims for some ill-defined concept of 'educational technology'. Loose promises can quickly result in the over-commitment of a unit, an inability to deliver the promised goods and a rapid loss of credibility.

Equally there is danger in the educational technologist starting from an apparently reasonable definition and laying claim to aspects of education which are regarded by others as their own province. Depending on the consensus of opinion within the institution, the educational technologist should be able to establish a working description of his field of operation which is as broad as the definitions cited at the beginning of this book. But he can only do this with the consent of those with whom he has to work. He cannot claim *sole* right to any aspect of educational practice. In practical terms he may have sole responsibility for the functional, operational aspects of his work.

It would therefore appear that in terms of organisation we should regard the educational technologist as having a function rather than a field. He does not have a field of study generated by himself and other educational technologists, but has borrowed and shared to create a related set of aspects of education that have sprung from media production, such as programmed learning, psychology, evaluation and methodology. Where the educational technologist has a clear role is in the bringing together and co-ordination of these formally disparate aspects. Now it is understandable that the specialists in each of the fields from which the borrowing has taken place should side with Richmond (1969) in asking why a new term 'educational technology' has to be invented. After all, is not what the educational technologist claims to be doing simply what is recognised by each specialist as good practice?

Here lies both the strength of the educational technologist's role and the starting point for a consideration of those things that have to be organised. The educational technologist enables a new technology, 'a change agent', to come into play by taking on a catalytic role. It is this recognition of 'good practice' from a wide range of skills that forms the new skills of the educational technologist within an institution. Havelock (1973) called him a 'knowledge broker' — he is that and more. Havelock also used the term 'linker' — he is that too, and more. I call him a 'mediator' in that he mediates the messages of others; he helps to apply form to content. He is expected to be manager, creative producer, pedagogue, psychologist, publicist, teacher, and to wear a whole host of other mantles. Ideally he is all of these in part but must be a manager most of all, for a good educational technologist must be able to apply management to other people's problems. He must be able to say 'I don't know' when the difficult questions are asked and not try to bluff. He can do this without loss of face and without the questioner's loss of faith because he must be able to add, 'I don't know, but I can find out the answer for you.' Then he has to find that answer. It is the skill of the educational technologist to be able to apply a systematic questioning to the questioner, to find out exactly what is required and then by an equally systematic approach to work out how to move towards some solution. In doing this the educational technologist is in a good position to relate to other professionals and apply their skill to others' problems. He must do this from the best organised base that can be built up within the institution.

Of what does this base consist? It should be built on organised resources that are readily brought to the service of all within that institution; resources so organised that the best use can be made of other resources outside the institution. There are two major sections of such a base. One is the ability to assist and support the development of curricula and courses throughout all departments, for here is the heart of the teaching/learning process. The second is the efficient organisation of the physical resources, both hardware and software, within the building.

What service can the educational technologist offer to those who are seeking educational development of some form? Later in this book we will be considering the question of the establishment of educational development for the teaching staff and learning development for the students. Obviously there are complex problems, involving as they do the interaction of individuals as professionals within their own fields.

From the service point of view the educational technologist should be able to offer to the rest of the staff within an institution an acceptable form of 'counselling' — a sort of educational psychiatrist's couch — whereby two or more people can help each other towards the best courses of action in the developing of new courses, new curricula and new materials. The strength of the educational technologist should be his *lack* of knowledge of the other person's subject content. What the educational technologist offers is a systematic approach from a new standpoint.

The educational technologist should be able to offer help by being in the first instance a neutral expert. This stance of neutrality is important if the relationship between the educational technology service and the potential client is to develop. Too often a rapid solution is found without proper analysis of the problems. In this case the chances of the solution being the best in the circumstances are about the same as in making an intelligent bet on a horse race. A 'client' who gets an unsatisfactory answer, or one which turns out to be inappropriate, is not just a client but is ammunition for anyone who wishes to oppose an educational technology service — a bonus for reaction.

Learn to Listen

If possible the educational technology unit should be a place to which people *want* to come, a place in which people can feel welcome, relaxed, unthreatened. One is not suggesting a haven of easy chairs within the austere confines of the institution, but a welcome and a willingness to listen are almost as good.

Then back up this welcome by *listening*. This is one of the key elements in the servicing of educational development, not just because it is polite and makes the client feel at ease, and not just because you have to find out what the question is before you can give an answer, but most of all because if you don't listen you won't hear the question that is *really* being asked. Naive as this may sound it is common to the experience of most people who provide services that clients rarely ask the question that they *should* ask. There is a great temptation when faced with an enquirer who has what appears to be a clear, well thought out enquiry to provide an answer to just that. It is all too easy to miss the more important issues which lie buried beneath that question.

Letting the enquirers talk and encouraging them to expand upon their needs should provide much more detail. You should be in possession of the context of the enquiry before ever approaching an answer.

Don't Assume Any Subject Knowledge

Whilst an understanding of the other person's subject content is an obvious advantage when two people converse and an ability to use the same vocabulary can remove misunderstandings, a display of one's own knowledge is not the purpose of the intercourse between educational technologist and 'client'. By assuming no knowledge of a subject a number of things follow. Firstly you will be placing yourself in a position similar to that of the student for whom the learning under discussion is to be designed. Secondly you will be able to ask questions from your position of 'ignorance' which, as we shall see, will most probably be of help to the enquirer to reformulate the questions. Thirdly, unless the academic field under discussion is actually your own discipline there is every possibility that an apparently communicative conversation may be working well at the level of denotation but may be failing at the important level of connotation. A careful assumption of ignorance is an important strategy in being able to serve effectively the educational needs of others.

If the enquirer presents a clear, reasonable statement of the problem then the provision of answers and assistance will be easy, especially if one takes the belief of the linguistic philosopher that a properly stated question contains within it the elements of the answer. However, despite the fact that we all consider the aims, objectives, methods and evaluation procedures when we contemplate the development of new curricula, it does not appear that these elements have always been fully considered by the time people realise that they have got a problem and go looking for help.

Learn to Ask Questions

Questioning is an art that needs practice. Everyone will develop methods that are best suited to their own personality. The aim should be to ask questions that cause the other person to reveal more about their enquiry, therefore one should try to avoid questions which can be answered by a simple 'yes' or 'no'. This would make for a very stilted conversation. Equally the questions should not be framed in inappropriate jargon. Each discipline has its own special language; to the initiated it is a precise tool which cuts away ambiguity and saves circumlocution, while to the uninitiated it is obscurantist verbiage which covers imprecise thinking and is a vehicle for elevating the ego. There can be few things more calculated to create resentment than the flaunting of 'jargon' in the wrong context. Educational technology, being a bastard child in the first place, has tended to borrow terminology like Autolycus, and is particularly prone to stealing from the pedagogue and the psychologist. It is amusing sometimes to listen to a mixed group using the same terms with obviously different meanings.

Learn to ask simple, clear questions. It will frighten the client less.

Find Out What Is Required

If the 'client' has not arrived with a clear breakdown of the problems at hand, try a process like this:

(a) What has to be learned?
(b) By whom has it to be learned?
(c) Why is it necessary — i.e. how does it fit into or develop out of the existing curriculum?
(d) How is this taught at the moment, or if it is new material how is it proposed that it will be learned?
(e) When is it required?

Now it is obvious that these questions are pointing towards a clarification of aims, objectives, methods and evaluation. The experience of virtually all those who are managing resource units in educational institutions shows that a surprisingly large number of people have not in fact asked themselves these elementary questions — at least not in these simple forms.

Academic staff have usually gained their positions by virtue of the excellence of their subject knowledge. This is perhaps most true of those who are charged with developing new courses and materials. They are expected to have greater knowledge because they have been involved at an academic level for a longer period of time, yet it is these very people who devise courses for those who are close to the beginning of their study. The gap between the knowledge held and the knowledge to be communicated is often enormous, and it is sometimes difficult for the expert to see things from the point of view of the first-year student. It can be a valuable duty of the educational technologist to bridge that gap through systematic posing of apparently simple questions.

In my own experience, which is similar to that of many resource providers, there have been many occasions on which this technique has been applied, resulting in a clear definition of the problem at hand, in which the academics have expressed some surprise at the simplicity of the process. Their surprise is increased when on reflection they realise that no one has asked such questions before, nor have they asked them of themselves.

The answers to the foregoing questions should begin to suggest to the educational technologist pedagogical methods that could be put forward for consideration. The methods and the subject will lead to consideration of appropriate media, and these together will suggest methods of assessment and evaluation.

Clearly the process is not quite as simple as this and requires knowledge and experience on the part of the educational technologist. Some of these elements will be dealt with later in this book, but for advice on aspects such as the selection of teaching/learning methods and the establishment of evaluation and assessment procedures the reader may look elsewhere within this series of books.

Find Out What Exists Already

Once a basis for proceeding has been agreed between the client and the educational technologist, the next step is to discover what already exists, what expertise is available or what assistance may be required.

We shall be dealing with 'information' in the next section of this book, but the point can be made here that education is taught with two lurking beasts — the 'reinvention of the wheel' and the 'not invented here' syndromes. Together they account for vast amounts of financial and human resources.

By finding out what already exists in terms of research, resources and expertise you can save for your client both time and money. If you can persuade him, and youself, that you don't have to make everything anew and that what other people have already done might be suitable (or possible to adapt to his needs), then you really will be enabling educational development. National agencies are constantly faced with demands for the creation of resources that already exist, and the same is true of individual institutions. A check of the commercial and non-commercial sources will often reveal that somebody has already produced the resource that you are about to make. There is no shame in buying in a product and releasing yourself to do other work.

The non-acceptance of other people's work can sometimes be seen in the field of research. There are still major basic research programmes being launched (in other countries of course) to discover when there is any value in programmed learning and microteaching. If research evidences duplication then it lags far behind the amount of duplication of effort in the production of learning resources. Even if one allows for the valuable learning that can take place in the process of creating these resources, there is still a crying need for the educational technologist to check carefully at the outset of a project that other people's time and money are not being wasted.

If the Parts of an Answer Exist, Bring Them Together

Having checked the appropriate sources of information and having found out that resources exist which might satisfy the enquirer, it should be the responsibility of the educational technologist to bring these resources together and present them in such a way that they either satisfy the client's need or else show clearly that with modification they can be used effectively.

Create the Resources

If having gone through this process there is still a need for the development of resources, course materials, research, etc., then you should be in a position to create the required resources, having in close co-operation with the client decided exactly what is required, having incorporated suitable existing materials, and thereby having identified the missing elements.

At this stage the choice is whether to make up the resources yourself or help the client towards a position in which he or she can make them.

This section set out to describe what is to be serviced with regard to the development of curricula and courses. By giving such a descriptive and perhaps prescriptive account we have seen that in the servicing of the ideas, the theoretical side of education, we can clearly define one of the functions of the educational technologist. He can, through the application of a systematic approach to other people's needs, provide a mechanism within the institution whereby people may be helped towards a solution of their developmental problems. In performing this function educational technology remains 'content-free', and by using the knowledge, expertise and information of others brings these elements together in such an ordered way as to provide the most reasonable, practical and economical solution to the problem posed.

Thus it can be stated that educational technology has a function, not a field.

In considering the provision of a service to colleagues within an institution one is faced with the unfortunate fact that no matter what one calls the unit that provides practical services (with the possible exception of calling it an 'education development unit'), it will be seen as the place that supplies audio-visual aids. To a great many teaching staff, 'audio-visual aids' are synonymous with 'educational first-aid', some sort of salve that is applied to the wound of teaching breakdown. Audio-visual aids are regarded as some kind of add-on feature, unessential, peripheral and dispensable. We who are involved in the creation and provision of learning materials should not be surprised by this attitude for we have used the term 'aid' for too long. We have provided neat packages which can be used or ignored at will, and we have been guilty of making glossily irrelevant materials for the sake of the gloss, rather than always aiming for the professionaly produced essential material that is tied to the heart of learning.

For the educational technology service to convince the sceptic that there is a role for the educational technologist in the shared effort of educational development, it is essential not only to provide services in a logical and systematically linked fashion, but to make this pattern obvious to all within the institution.

The logic of developmental need leading to practical solution suggests that the educational technology service must provide practical assistance on three levels — information, software, and hardware.

These are, after all, the stages through which the teacher should go when approaching each new teaching/learning problem. We have dealt briefly with the question of helping the enquirer towards the clear definition of the problem. Ideally the teacher will always delineate the aims and objectives (what was some years ago referred to as the 'underware') before proceeding to discover what software is available to enable him to reach those objectives. Once appropriate software has been secured or created then the question can be considered of the hardware which is necessary to enable that software to be used. In reality the process is rarely so ordered. Decisions on software are modified by knowlege of the hardware that is already available. There is no point in proceeding to develop a learning programme that is dependent upon the use of computers if there is no chance of getting access to such machinery.

However, such are the pressures on teaching staff, so unused are they to utilising an effective support staff, that all too often the decisions about which materials to incorporate in new teaching programmes are based first of all on the equipment that is available and with which the teacher is familiar. Coupled with this is the use of materials that have been used before, whether they are ideally suited for the task in hand or not. The end result is that the availability of equipment becomes the starting point for decision-making, rather than the educational objectives — a mechanical tail wagging an educational dog.

However much one may criticise this approach to the selection of learning resources, it is at least more open-minded than the outright rejection of audio-visual materials and the close adherence to chalk and the instructional mode. If the educational technologist believes that amongst the alternative methodologies and the broad spectrum of media there are combinations which might be more appropriate for the particular learning context, then it is up to him to create an affective change amongst his colleagues. If they are resistant to suggestions of change who can blame them — they find security in using those media and methods with which they are familiar. If what they do is successful what right has the educational technologist to suggest that there is something better? A direct approach is likely to force the sceptic back into the entrenched position of the conservative for whom 'if it *need* not be changed, then it *must* not be changed'.

The educational technologist must first of all work to create the climate within which this affective change towards an acceptance of possible alternatives can take place.

Through the educational technology service the staff should have easy access to information; first of all to current information on research and opinion, as the expert who has been published may be more ready believed than the man on the spot. This will require close co-operation with library staff. Secondly, there should be as rapid access as possible to information on software. This is essential if the client is to be persuaded that there *are* materials that might meet the present needs. Again this will require co-operation with the library staff. Thirdly, there must be a soundly based information service on hardware. Although decisions on hardware should be well down the order of priorities, when that point is reached the decisions are crucial, costly, and have long-term effects.

If the educational technologist in concert with others can develop within the institution reliable information services then there is a good foundation for the creation of trust. From trust the change can grow.

The next service must be that of providing software. If the 'client', having gathered the appropriate information, now seeks the learning materials there should be an easy system whereby:

(a) it can be ascertained whether appropriate materials are available within the institution, and whether they can be used;
(b) if they are not available within the institution there is a process whereby they can be bought, hired or borrowed;
(c) if they do not appear to exist or are not obtainable a process can be initiated whereby they can be created.

The final aspect of the service should be that concerned with hardware. Obviously the question of hardware must have been considered before the client sets about obtaining software, so that the occasion should not arise in which someone reaches the final stage — that of presentation — only to face the frustration of finding that the equipment does not exist, is unavailable or does not work. The educational technologist should be able to establish a measure of control whereby the equipment within an insitution, or that to be bought in, is co-ordinated, maintained and used in the most efficient way both educationally and economically.

None of the foregoing suggestions presupposes any particular pattern. Centralised or decentralised organisation may be appropriate depending on the institution. Managerial control by a single unit or shared co-operation between several departments may be equally suitable. Later sections of this book will examine some of the issues raised. What we have now considered is that the educational technologist should be able to provide within the institution a range of services, namely: advice and consultation, information, software and hardware. Now it might well be argued that the second of these is the responsibility of the library and the third and fourth can be done by any audio-visual unit or media department. It might also be argued that if all the educational technologist does is provide a range of services, and in doing so takes a responsive rather than an innovative role, why call himself an educational technologist? Why lay claims to what other people can do? What I am arguing is that by providing such services the educational technologist:

(a) satisfies existing educational needs;
(b) assists in the identification of latent needs;
(c) creates in a controlled way a climate in which change can flourish;

(d) creates circumstances in which innovation can take place through co-operation rather than through threat or coercion.

The complete chain from advice to material provision is not some adjunct to the educational technologist's 'technology' — it *is* the basis of that technology.

The psychologist has as much to give to educational development as does the media producer, the curriculum developer and the host of researchers. They bring to educational development their own professional skills. By being thoroughly professional in his service role the educational technologist can, together with these other professionals, generate innovation, creativity and educational development. In addition, the educational technologist may himself possess any of these other skills.

4 INFORMATION

'Your decisions are only as good as your information' — Educational Product Information Exchange, Institute of New York.

With any educational institution from the primary school upwards, one of the crucial factors in organisation and management of resources — perhaps *the* most crucial factor — is information. One must have information on the elements that make up the totality of what has to be managed. That which is not known cannot be controlled.

Why should there be control of information? Certainly not with any view to censorship or empire-building. Let us start from the simplest examples. The lack of information on available software can rob a learning situation of just that resource which would bring it to life and fix it in the minds of the learners. In the case of secondary education the example is often quoted of the class that is just about to start a study of the Brontës as part of the English course. Let us suppose that the school is situated in a city a hundred miles or more from the bleak countryside round Haworth. There is no way for the teacher to know whether all or most of the pupils have a broadly common conception of the context in which the novels were written. In the classroom down the corridor is the geography department which contains a filmstrip of the Yorkshire moors. It has, perhaps, not been used for some time because the curriculum has changed and the filmstrip is no longer considered suitable. The filmstrip now lies in a drawer. Yet this is just the visual stimulus that is needed by the English class. Five or ten minutes' viewing would set the subsequent programme in a context which some would term 'meaningful'; but the English teacher doesn't even know that it exists.

Because of the lack of an organised system he is not trained, nor does he expect, to look for resources in other places. The geography teacher has never realised that other people might want to use the resources in his department. Nowhere in the school is there any record into which the information about that filmstrip could be entered, or in which the English teacher could have searched. The opportunity for a small but significant piece of learning has been unused.

It does not require much imagination to think of situations in which material from one department can meet the teaching needs of another.

The more obvious examples are those which provide background information, a context for another subject. If one can think of just a few examples and then multiply these by the number of classes, the number of departments and the number of institutions, it soon becomes apparent that there is an appalling potential for missed opportunities. This of course assumes that every teacher is fully aware of the resources that are to hand within his or her *own* room and department.

Quite seriously, there is a clear case for the control of information on resources. Various methods will be considered later and the advantages of such control examined in greater detail.

The case of the filmstrip lying forgotten in the geography department (apologies to geographers — they are usually amongst the best users of resources) highlights the function of information control which can often be hidden by the practical details of any particular case. That the pupils were unable to see the filmstrip is unfortunate but it is not necessarily serious. After all, a great deal of literary study has been done, and is being done, with recourse to visual aids. The point that is perhaps more serious is that without the knowledge of that potential resource the teacher was not in a position to make certain crucial decisions about the content of the lesson, the methodology to be employed and even the objectives of that part of the course. Some might argue that he is better off not having been called on to make such decisions, but if, knowing of the existence of such a filmstrip and having considered the implications and the possible gains and losses, the teacher decided *not* to use it, then he might be making a positive selection of what might be called a 'traditional' method. The decision will have been made in the light of the information, not in ignorance of it.

This is a simple, possibly simplistic, case and one does not want to make too much of it. However if one raises the level of the choices and decisions to, say, the planning of new courses, the setting of new objectives or new assessment standards, if one is considering the equipping of a department or an institution with long-term goals, then any gaps in the information can be critical in the decision-making process and can seriously damage future activities.

What then is the current state of information control — is there any need to make a case for the inclusion of this within the professional concerns of the educational technologist? One can see in other areas of education that not only is there a high degree of information control, but also that everyone takes it for granted that this should be so.

For example there can be few, if any, institutions of further and higher education which, having a collection of books, have not employed one or more professional librarians to look after them. The expectation of the library user is that there will be an easy system of reference to lead to the books which contain the knowledge sought. One also expects the system to let one know if that book is available and, having found this out, one expects to find the book in good condition on the right place on the right shelf. If any of these elements fail our expectation we judge that the librarian is failing to fulfil his or her professional duties. Because of the pressure that we, the users, can apply on the professionals and because they are just that — professionals — we have a vast library system which, aside from the odd quirks, works very well. In institutions the size of universities one can expect to find libraries of books, journals and papers in almost every department and the expectation is there that these will be as efficiently run as the largest of the libraries.

Similar systems of control can be found in the management of institutions, in course content, in student monitoring, in the ordering and using of supplies. Why then in institution after institution can one find no record of the audio-visual equipment that is available, no record of the learning resources, no record of the new materials being purchased or used, and no record of materials that are available outside the institution?

Considering the management of the institution the case is clear — people are paid to do the job. There must be strict data control if an institution of several hundreds or thousands of people is to be run. Just imagine the effect of having no data by which to draw up the staff salaries. There may be no record of the number and location of projectors but it is relatively certain that there will be a record of the number and location of staff. Money and holding on to one's own job are highly rated by industrial trainers as motivating factors.

In the case of course content, teachers, tutors and lecturers maintain a high level of awareness of what is happening within their own field — at least in terms of what is written. As well as a professional concern for the subject one of the major motivating factors for staff as well as students must be the fact that at the end of a unit of time an examination has to be sat by the student. This may be an unsubstantiated assertion, but whether from an ethical concern for the students' success or from the need to maintain a 'pass rate', many teachers acknowlege that examinations are a highly motivating factor.

The record-keeping on students, from attendance to performance levels, is highly organised and the use of consumable supplies is eventually subject to the scrutiny of auditors.

In all these cases professional skills are recognised and employed. Yet at the same time there are areas in which it is acknowledged that there is a need for a serious look at information control. There has recently been considerable investment in computerised data retrieval related to courses, in an attempt to improve the guidance that is given to prospective students in order to find training that matches their aspirations and aptitudes. Here again professional skills are being employed to enable individuals to make better choices.

Many colleges, polytechnics and universities do have co-ordinated information systems relating to audio-visual aids and the other matters that come under the broad umbrella of 'educational technology', but many have only partial control; there may even be some with no control system at all. My case is that, just as in the examples already cited in which need is matched with professional skill, the educational technologist should make it part of his or her professional pride to assist in the efficient management of information.

In making such a statement one must stress the word 'assist', for immediately one considers the sort of data that have to be controlled one is immediately in danger of being seen to be encroaching on the provinces of other people. It is therefore necessary to examine each of the sectors of data, place each in the context of the institution and balance the interest of the educational technologist with the roles of the other people involved.

Information and the Librarian

Libraries have been organising the knowledge that is carried by the printed word for centuries. During that time systems have been evolved by which we, the seekers after knowledge, can with little difficulty search through catalogue systems for things of whose existence we are are ignorant. A crude and ill-defined subject concept can, through the refining process of classification systems, be converted into specific references leading us to books and journals which meet our needs.

The user is not, and perhaps should never be, aware of the amount of work that has gone into the creation of that system. The easier it is to operate the better for the customer, yet the library catalogue is a good example of a system in which the greater the sophistication of the input the greater is the likelihood of an easy and accurate final result for the user.

We should, therefore, be eager to use the skills of the librarian in information control in areas other than books. We would not think of arbitrarily deciding that a certain range of illnesses should be treated by the medical profession and that we should invent a new type of profession to treat another arbitrarily selected set. Of course within the medical profession there are specialists, but so there are amongst librarians.

Recent years have seen the introduction of courses in 'non-book media librarianship' in virtually all the British library schools, and increasingly there are in-service courses for qualified librarians who completed their training days when there were few if any non-book media. There is no need here to consider in any detail the exact methods employed by librarians for classifying, cataloguing and indexing materials. Norman Beswick and many others have written lucidly on this subject.

However, there is one argument that is central to the majority of the recent writing about the bibliographic control of non-book media and it is worthy of our consideration, for although the educational technologist, the resource organiser, will not normally be required to have library skills, an appreciation of the basis on which the librarian works is essential for intelligent and sympathetic co-operation.

The main force of this argument is against the invention of new systems for controlling information. The method by which the information is recorded may differ, and this will be considered shortly, but when considering the classification and cataloguing of non-book media one has to question the apparent need to invent a system which is different from that used to classify and catalogue books just because the object to be recorded does not look like a book. A film, a set of slides, or a learning pack are clearly different from a book in many ways. They are physically different, they require different storage and one must have equipment with which to access the information that they hold. Yet at the same time these learning materials have many similarities with books, and it is these similarities which should be considered.

This is best illustrated by the set of examples given by Malcolm Shiffrin. Take a book. It has a title, an index, a list of contents and probably some illustrations. It is bound in covers and has certain dimensions. All these attributes, together with a brief description of the subject matter, make up the catalogue entry with which we are familiar in our book libraries. Added to this may be a number indicating classification under one of the schemes such as Dewey or the Universal Decimal Classification. If the back is removed from the book and we are left with a package of illustrations and text, the content has remained the same — only the physical form has changed. Assume now that the illustrations and some of the textual ideas are transferred to slides or filmstrip. The title, contents list, text, and index may be carried in an accompanying booklet or may be recorded on an audio-tape or audio cassette. Basically the content remains the same but already we can see that there are alternative physical forms which can carry that content. The example can easily be extended to other forms. A camera can be moved over the illustrations to produce a ciné film or a video-tape. Different media can be selected as being the most appropriate for different sections of the work and we end up with a mixed media package.

In each case the only element that differs from the cataloguing of the book is the description of the physical form. Certainly there may be forms which begin to change the original concept. Dramatisation or documentary reconstruction of a text may demand alteration in the detail of the entry, but the book librarian has always had to face this in the case of plays made from novels or translations from one language to another.

As a result one should be able to envisage a catalogue in which there is a common style of entry for any item.

The elements would be:-

Number

TITLE

Author statement (if applicable)

Description of contents

Physical form designation: extent: enrichment

There may be variations to this depending upon the detailed rules preferred or the format eventually chosen as the universal library standard, but the basic principle remains the same. With this in mind one once again questions the need felt very strongly by some people to invent new systems.

If books and non-books (a term which one sincerely hopes will become redundant in a few years' time) are catalogued by the same system several advantages follow immediately.

The combined cataloguing of learning materials with books should convey to the user the concept that each of these items is a carrier of information. This will be less strong as a 'message' if the book and non-book records are separated, but if the same method is used the similarity should carry its own significance.

The combined cataloguing has the function of modifying the search strategy of the user. If each medium is catalogued separately it is normal for the user to have decided on the medium required before a subject search is started. For example the user may have set out to look for a set of slides on a particular topic, and if there is a catalogue of slide sets he may or may not find something suitable. There is nothing inherent in the system of separate catalogues that will automatically send the searcher across to another file.

On the other hand the searcher using a combined catalogue and seeking a set of slides on a particular subject may, on opening the file at the appropriate point, find that in addition to slide sets there are several films, a couple of simulation exercises and a set of work cards which will serve his teaching or learning needs. At this point the user may be stimulated to re-examine the methodologies to be used in the teaching/learning. Because the medium *does* affect the message the presentation of alternative media by the combined catalogue raises important questions about the objectives already formulated by the searcher. As a result there may be either a choice of a more appropriate resource than had at first been sought, or even a refinement of the objectives.

To construct such a catalogue is a highly skilled job. The better and more professional the input into the catalogue the more accurate and easy to use it will be for the ordinary enquirer. One cannot stress too highly the need for the control of information about the whole range of learning resources to be placed in the hands of qualified librarians. The relationship between the educational technologist and the librarian in the overall context of the organisation and management of resources within the institution is therefore of crucial importance.

The catalogue can itself be a teaching tool. And the form of the tool is of some importance to the user. In purchasing a product we normally consider whether it is of familiar construction, whether it is easy to use, whether we can get spare parts, and whether one has to learn new skills in order to use it effectively. The same can be said of the library catalogue. I do not propose to go over the different methods in detail, as it is for those who operate within institutions to decide which physical system is best for the particular circumstances. As has already been noted there is ample guidance to be had from Beswick *et al.* From a personal point of view as a 'user' the fact that information *is* organised is the most important fact. The system and how it is constructed is of less importance as long as I can see how to *use* it. The way that the data is presented is of less importance than the system.

Like everybody else I have preferences and dislikes when I become a consumer. When using a catalogue I don't see why I should have to learn a new system for non-books after 'they' have spent such a long time getting me used to the book catalogue. I like library cards, they are easy to scan and one can search rapidly. I can understand pictures which tell me what the medium is on each card, but get confused over colours. There aren't enough colours that are easily distinguishable on cards to identify the forty-three media that can be found in the library (and in any case the cards that are on sale this year are not quite the same shades as last year's). I don't see why I should have to learn a new set of key words for non-book media when the books are still being classified and catalogued in the established way. I always thought that the indexing terms on the cards in the classified file were 'key words' in any case. I like the integration of media and books in one file because it keeps leading me to discoveries of new sources and resources. On the other hand, as a believer in Murphy's Law ('anything that can go wrong, will go wrong') I always find that the edge-notched cards are torn, the needle for the punched cards is bent, and the little holes in the Optional Co-incidence Cards are blocked with Tippex and the crumbs from the previous user's sandwiches. This however is only a personal view!

Librarians working within an educational institution often face difficulties, finding themselves torn between a series of conflicting interests. In the very large institutions, universities and the larger polytechnics, the sheer size of the library is sufficient to give it strength. It can exist as a major component within the complex inter-departmental stucture. Libraries in small institutions may not have this degree of independence and may begin to feel more acutely the pressures that can be applied by other professional interests. It is not the point of this book to present arguments about who should select books and other media. The case for subject specialist influence on the choice of related learning materials must be a strong one. Whether the resource holdings of an institution should be centralised or dispersed is a very different question from that which asks whether the library should be centrally controlled or fragmented into departmental holdings outside the organisational control of the libary staff.

The educational technologist in his role of resource organiser will be concerned with the promotion of the best use of existing resources, the assistance of others in the selection of new resources, and the production of audio-visual materials. It is, therefore, natural to find many an organiser who has strong ideas about how such media should be arranged. If such materials are to be made available to staff and/or students the educational technologist should be concerned about the way in which the materials are used and also that they *are* available, but the way in which they are stored and accessed is within the professional province of the librarian. Once a user has collected the desired materials then in many cases there will be a need to use equipment, a need which is within the province of the 'resource organiser'. Thus it is clear that virtually irrespective of the particular managerial pattern that is evolved the two professional interests are inseparably intertwined once non-book media are introduced.

The librarian should not be expected to be the educational technologist, nor should the educational technologist be expected to be the librarian. Co-operation is essential and this is more likely to grow from a mutual understanding of the objectives of both jobs and the systems which are desirable to achieve those objectives, than from a jealous guarding of territorial rights. Whatever the official relationship in hierarchical or committee terms between the educational technologist and the librarian, a recognition that in the areas of overlap they have many aims in common will help to achieve a sound working relationship. Both desire (a) that the teacher and learner should be able to discover with ease the data on appropriate resources; (b) that such resources should then be as readily available as is practicable; and (c) that circumstances should be created in which there are as few difficulties as possible in using these resources.

Information on Hardware Purchase

Consideration will be given later to the physical control of 'hardware'. Information about equipment in general is an essential component of the organisation of resources.

As has been noted earlier there are many within education who will turn to the educational technologist (no matter what title is given to or assumed by him) as the man who deals with audio-visual aids. Though this is a heavy cross to bear most of the time it can be the first point in a fruitful dialogue. If a colleague enquires about a piece of equipment this may be the entrée into a discussion of course content and learning methods. It may even be a covert opportunity for staff development. On the other hand the enquiry is just as likely to be genuinely about equipment — its potential, its availability and cost. In both cases the educational technologist must be in a position to give as accurate an answer as possible — and here is the real difficulty.

The amount of equipment available within the blanket term 'audio-visual aids' is enormous. At the time of writing the equipment file at the Scottish Council for Educational Technology contains information on approximately 10,000 items of audio-visual equipment available in the UK, and it is clear that this is not entirely complete and up-to-date. Given that the range of equipment is of this order and that the speed with which manufacturers change models is apparently ever-increasing, then there is little chance for the resource organiser to maintain his personal file on equipment. Nor, I would suggest, should the individual ever attempt to do this. There are a number of national bodies in the UK such as SCET and NCAVAE who have devoted much time and effort to building such files. Most other countries have similar national institutions which have performed similar functions. To strive to duplicate such major collections of data in any single institution would be a waste of energy verging on the criminal.

The first requisite for the resource organiser is to know where the nearest effective source of such information exists and how best to access the required data. There is a natural inclination for anyone who is likely to be in the position of answering such questions to deal with a limited range of equipment from a small selection of manufacturers: A neat collection of catalogues with which one is familiar is a comfort, but it can become a deceptive crutch. An institution may have a controlled policy of equipment purchase, limiting the types of machinery in order to maximise the cost effectiveness of spares and maintenance. This in itself is wholly admirable but can be a two-edged sword. The equating of equipment held with the level of information that should be accessible can lead to a number of serious constraints.

In the first place purchasing policy may need regular updating to keep pace with market changes. Secondly a rigid adherence to a purchasing policy and, therefore, to a limitation on the information provided, may dissuade the information provider from widening the search for data to include an item of equipment not previously considered appropriate but which may now be exactly right to meet the newly articulated objectives of a colleague. Thirdly, access to the totality of equipment information may change policies and strategies within the institution. For example the development of new species of hardware may suggest the alteration of amortisation periods for equipment already held. It is equally possible that equipment innovation may radically alter notions of equipment systems. The recent improvements in colour video equipment have resulted in major reassessments of institutional film-making capacities — and this in a sector of the market that is, perhaps, changing more rapidly than any other. The promises that are held out to us by the micro-chip and the effective reduction in cost of high-expenditure items such as television cameras could well result in sweeping changes.

Much of this will be missed if the resource organiser maintains his or her equipment information only at the level of what is now known within the institution. One must always be ready to search in areas of information that are unknown rather than staying within the safety of the known. The latter leads to ossification.

In this sense information plays a crucial role in the decision-making process. Decisions for purchase need to be assisted with a 'best buy' type of service. Now there is no way that a major information base could be expected to provide 'best buy' information unless all institutions were identical. Any data service worth its salt will attempt to isolate the criteria by which the enquirer will eventually choose the item of hardware. In effect, because each enquiry springs from individual circumstances each with its own defining parameters, an information service will attempt to produce a different 'best buy' to match each enquiry. By the same light the resource organiser should be able to dissect each hardware question within the institution to discover the criteria for the request. It is a well recognised phenomenon that this process often leads away from the original question to other, perhaps more suitable, items of equipment, to considerations of alternative software differing from that which is implicit in the hardware enquiry, and even to considerations of alternative teaching/learning methods.

The more accurate the analytical method developed by the resource organiser, the better will be the search criteria for the request to the larger data base and hence the more satisfactory will be the final answer.

As a general guide it is perhaps wise to be cautious about every enquiry for information about hardware. Be reluctant to take any question at its face value. This in no way suggests that one should insult the intelligence of the enquirer by indicating that they don't know what they should be asking for.

Information on Software Held within the Institution

The case has already been presented for the standardisation of the *method* of recording information about software, and the value that can be gained from having a unified catalogue. The task of creating that catalogue is properly the province of the librarian but the organisation of the software record and its place within the institution is, in many cases, the responsibility of the educational technologist.

As has been shown a properly constructed catalogue can be a strong influence upon search strategies and therefore can alter the whole educational process. It ought to be a matter of concern to all who are involved in the organisational pattern that this power to change is used to the best effect, to create desired outcomes, not simply to create change for its own sake. The software data should therefore be efficacious rather than simply effective.

The first organisational criterion is accessibility. How can the information be made most readily available to anyone, staff or student, who is seeking data, and what are the problems that have to be faced? An immediate thought is to collect together the information on *all* the items of software held within the institution, to catalogue it according to a simple set of rules and to make one central file open to all. Logical though this answer might appear, its practicality must be called into question. To begin with, if there is no formal record of the non-book media in existence, one should not underestimate the amount of time that is required to catalogue and classify these items. The production of the catalogue record by card, by fiche or any other method also takes time and manpower. If a librarian is being asked to make a reasonably full entry for each item, and to classify and cross-reference each entry, then a rate of forty to fifty completed items per week per librarian would be a very acceptable input rate. The complete cataloguing of an institution's software holdings might take a considerable time to build up to a usable record.

A small college might find it possible to build such a record under central control. Here it would be accessible to all staff just as the library has always been. Many a college already has a library and resource centre combined into one facility. In most of these the catalogues are either combined as one or are situated close together.

However, a spot check around a number of colleges shows that whilst the catalogue in this resource library lists the items on its own shelves, there is no record of the undeniably large number of items that are held within the various departments. No matter how good the library catalogue is, under these circumstances it will never give more than a partial answer to anyone seeking resources within the college.

Library staff are charged with maintaining a record of the items directly within their control. To suggest that they now extend their remit to include the cataloguing of all the other non-book material in the college will increase the work load to such an extent that it will probably be beyond the capability of the library staff. This may appear to be an insoluble dilemma, but it is not impossible to resolve. Careful discussion with the librarians can secure their support for this important development. It may be possible to organise the flow of information to the librarians in such a way that they are not overwhelmed. If the departments of the college can be persuaded of the eventual benefit of a central record they can simplify the task of the librarians by providing a complete list of the items they hold. If this can be done by means of a pro-forma document then the effort required from each department can be minimised and the work of the librarians eased. The exact structure of a suitable pro-forma document will depend upon the way in which the particular library prefers to file the data. The layout shown on p. 52 is a suggested approach.

Despite the apparent complexity of this form each item will only take two or three minutes to complete. Take any non-book item and try filling out a form. With practice and only a little training a member of the clerical staff can do much of this work.

For such a strategy to work there must be complete agreement between all the parties concerned. This may take time and tact to secure. It is also important to note that this exercise will be a commitment extending over many months or even years until the retrospective catalogue is completed. Once the record has been brought up to date it will be a relatively simple job to maintain the file on new materials. Though such form-filling smacks of bureaucracy it need not take up a great deal of time and can become as automatic, on the arrival or creation of new learning materials, as the filling in of the copyright forms by the side of the photocopier.

Larger institutions, those with departmental libraries of any size, may prove to be unsuitable for a policy of a single centralised catalogue. Universities and polytechnics are frequently equipped with subject libraries, each staffed by professionals. Each of these should

Media Cataloguing Pro-forma.	*Circle or underline appropriate sub-headings*
SUBJECT AREAS	
TITLE SUB TITLE AUTHOR/CREATOR	SERIES.
DISTRIBUTION COMPANY	PLACE | YEAR
AVAILABLE FOR PREVIEW FROM	TERMS OF AVAILABILITY
MEDIUM INFORMATION	Single Unit/Multi Media Module | IF MODULE, MEDIA INVOLVED. (Ref. nos. only)
1. PRINT MATERIAL	Booklet/Worksheet/Information Sheets/Sheet music/Artwork posters/Photographs.
2. FILMSTRIP	Single frame/Double Frame. No. of frames b & w./colour.
3. OHP TRANSPARENCY	No. of frames . Overlays/Masking. Size x b & w./Colour.
4. SLIDE	Single frame/Double frame. No. in set. Mount type. Size x . b & w./colour.
5. FILM	Reel/Cassette/Loop. 8mm/Super 8mm/16mm/35mm. Sound/Silent Optical/Magnetic Speed: x f.p.s. Playing time: b & w./colour.
6. VIDEO	Tape/Cassette. Tape width: Machine make/type
7. SOUND TAPE	Reel/Cassette/Cartridge. 2/4 Tracks. Mono/Stereo If Pulsed, System: Speed of recording/playback: Playing time:
8. SOUND DISC.	Playing speed: Size: Mono/Stereo/Quad. If set, no. of sides: No. of tracks: Total playing time:
9. OTHER ITEMS.	
SUMMARY OF CONTENTS	
TECHNICAL QUALITY	
SUGGESTED LEVEL(S) OF USE	Infants/Primary/Middle/L Secondary/S. Secondary/Further Education.
EDUCATIONAL EVALUATION	
SUGGESTED AMENDMENTS/ ADDITIONS	
FURTHER RELEVANT MATERIAL	
ANY FURTHER COMMENTS.	
REPORT FILED BY	EDUCATIONAL ESTABLISHMENT | DATE

of course have a record of their non-book as well as their book holdings. It is worth finding out the extent to which they have any records of the media held by staff members. Again a small sampling of departments tends to suggest that there is remarkably little knowledge of what is held. The reasons given are, as one might expect, the normal ones of (a) there are not enough staff to keep the record; (b) the materials belong to the individual staff members; (c) why would anyone not studying this particular part of this particular subject be interested in my materials; and (d) if we need something extra we have a good idea what Joe or Fred has, and anyway we can ask. All of these are given as honest reasons for not having a list. But Joe or Fred could be run over by a bus or be offered a job elsewhere. When they leave does all the knowledge go with them? Have you ever had the experience of cleaning out a colleague's room and finding *all* those teaching materials just lying there? As to their subject-specific nature, no one will ever have the chance to discover whether any of the materials held within another department are of any use to them unless they have access to the relevant information.

If each department within the polytechnic or university can make its own catalogue — a job requiring all the persuasive skills of the educational technologist — then by this division of work it should be possible to collect together copies of each of the departmental records into a central index. It is at this point that the searcher can begin to cross subject and departmental boundaries.

Such a development would be assisted if each departmental library automatically deposited copies of its record cards in a central base. However, although there is enough evidence to convince one that this would result in a greater utilisation of resources, an enlivening of learning through the alternation of different teaching methods, and a revelation of the amount of duplicated material held within any institution, it has to be acknowledged that this would require a great deal of manpower, particularly in the early stages. It might be argued that such an effort would be disproportionate to the amount of use that the suggested record would have.

If I want to catch a train from A to B, I look in the railway timetable — which took a lot of money and effort to put together — knowing that it will help me not only in this instance, but also if I want to go somewhere other than B, or to reach B by a different route. More importantly the existence of the timetable in all its complexity shows me that there are other places and other routes. It must also be of help to those running the railways when they want to contemplate any changes to the system. Similarly, the potential usefulness of a central catalogue may not be immediately apparent when its creation is first contemplated.

It will be up to the educational technologist to discuss the possibility of catalogue building with the library staff, and the task may well be judged too big for the expected returns. At some stage there comes a moment at which decisions have to be made on faith, for it is difficult to make clear, objective judgements on the basis of possible future returns and changing situations.

Information on Hardware Held within the Institution

If you can, ignore reality for a few minutes, put aside the issue of the actual management of the equipment within the institution and consider only the problem of information about that equipment. This may seem like a fatuous exercise. 'Why not get on with looking after the damned stuff, instead of fretting about with silly cards covered in information?' This sort of remark is usually delivered with a disdain that only comes from years of practice, well larded with ignorance. The confidence with which it is delivered increases with the social nature of the occasion. It is said so often that it is all too easy for the hard-pressed staff member who is charged with looking after the equipment to be eventually persuaded to accept the apparent validity of the remark.

How can one set about organising equipment before finding out what exists? One cannot organise what one does not know. A recent survey by the SCET Resource Liaison Project, 1977-9, has demonstrated that school-teachers say that the biggest block to the use of audio-visual materials is the problem of the equipment. They can't get it, it doesn't work or they can't use it. Whether this is true or not, it is what they *say*. A survey of Further Education Colleges in Scotland tended to suggest that equipment problems were given a high priority by those with an educational technology responsibility. It has been observed that, in a distorted corollary of Parkinson's Law, equipment problems expand to fill all the available time. This may be a reflection of the situation in which, lacking support staff and sufficient time, the resource organiser does not have the confidence to tackle the broader issues of 'educational technology' — especially those involving the human and pedagogical aspects. It can be argued that control of information on the hardware, though time-consuming in the early stages, can lead to a situation which is virtually self-sustaining, thus in the longer term making the job much easier.

Let us take the problem in stages. Before attempting to come to any decisions about the management of the equipment itself, find the answers to the following questions:-

(a) What equipment exists in the institution?
(b) Where is it located?
(c) Who 'owns' it?
(d) What uses does it have?
(e) What state of repair is it in?

What Equipment Exists in the Institution?

How many people know how much equipment actually exists within their institution? If you do then you are in the minority, one of a privileged few. The reasons given for not knowing are many and complex, the one most often advanced being that the organiser has enough trouble trying to satisfy the customers' needs from his own supply of equipment without having to bother with poking his nose into other people's affairs. There are two answers to this: firstly that some of the difficulties may arise from not having a sufficiently large pool of equipment with which to meet the demands placed upon the service, in which case a knowledge of what exists elsewhere in the building may on occasion provide the required answer; and secondly that possessing information about equipment held by other members of staff does not necessarily imply any intrusion into their territorial domain against their will.

There are hosts of horror stories about the equipment that has eventually been found when a thorough inventory has been attempted. The aforementioned cine-camera strapped to the microscope had a little plaque on it indicating that it was part of a bequest to a medical department. It could not therefore be removed, despite the fact that it was sufficiently sophisticated to be used by a fully professional film unit yet was only used for single-frame shooting. Each person seems to have stories of finding equipment locked away unused in cupboards, sometimes even in its original packing cases. The reasons given range from the excuse that it was somebody else who ordered it and it doesn't suit the currently preferred teaching methods, to the extreme of 'Well, it's expensive and it might get damaged if it is used.'

All of the above cases are true, only the institutions are kept anonymous to protect the guilty. One factor does emerge and that is that individuals are sensitive about such issues, and must therefore be approached with caution and tact.

To discover what equipment exists, it would be a good safeguard to obtain the sanction of the Director or Principal. The argument for an inventory can be clearly stated on the grounds of economics. If money has been spent on audio-visual equipment then it is reasonable to suggest that the most effective use is made of such equipment. No planning can take place without an inventory. The support of the Principal should not be used as a battering ram to beat down the doors of obstinate departments, but rather as an indication of support for a strategy designed for the general good. There should be no suggestion that the gathering of information means 'taking' equipment away from anybody. If people are prepared or can be persuaded to co-operate they may be led to see that the willingness to share what they hold, should the need arise, can be rewarded by access to equipment held by others.

Therefore it is worth trying to take an inventory of all the items of equipment. In the first stage do no more than this, grouping equipment under generic headings such as film projectors, slide projectors, tape recorders, etc. This will at least give an indication of the scale of the equipment holding before any conclusions are reached as to the best method of using it.

Where is Equipment Located?

The inventory should contain data on the location of equipment. The level of detail required to make this information useful will vary according to the size of the institution. If we are to be able to use this information as a planning tool when we come to consider the management of the resources, then different levels of detail may be required. In a small college it may be sufficient to know that there is a film projector of a certain make in the history department, for that may refer to four rooms on a particular corridor. In a university the department of history may occupy five separate houses, scattered around a campus or throughout a town, each house having several floors and many staircases.

The objects of the exercise are to identify the location of equipment so that in the short term a request can be made for the loan of equipment from one department to another should the need arise. In the longer term the location will be useful in deciding what possible patterns of equipment organisation can be put forward for consideration by colleagues. The present position of equipment may tend to suggest leaving each piece where it is but creating a 'free-flow' so that each item can be borrowed when required, or perhaps grouping equipment into nodes to service a number of rooms, or alternatively forming a central pool of all the equipment and spares. The first has the advantage of causing the least disturbance but makes any regular maintenance of the equipment extremely difficult. The third, at the other end of the scale, makes control and maintenance relatively easy but creates distribution problems. (This will be dealt with in more detail in the next section of the book.)

The known geography of the institution can then be put against the equipment location list. Without any formal plans any resource organiser should be able to deduce the ease or difficulty with which equipment can be moved. The distance between buildings should be known. Are there lifts or will gear have to be carried downstairs? If trollies are to be used are there ramps, and can door sills be avoided? Even if no organisational changes can be made, there is at least the chance of introducing periodic checks on the state of equipment. If by doing this small thing you can reduce the number of times that staff find equipment which doesn't work, then the collection of this information may be instrumental in changing people's confidence in, and therefore attitude towards, audio-visual aids.

Who 'Owns' Equipment?

Simply because equipment is to be found within an institution and that institution has a formal governing structure, it cannot be assumed that everything belongs to the institution. When it does, in most cases the equipment belongs to the institution itself and not the individual, but to state this realistically would upset a great many people and create resentments which could work against the efficiency of a support service. There are cases in schools of rather draconian measures being taken with regard to equipment (Lewis, 1973). The direct line of authority from the Director of Education to the head-teacher may make it possible for the staff to be ordered to bring all their audio-visual equipment and materials to the school hall, but it is doubtful whether a similar 'order' within a college or university would meet with the same degree of success achieved by Basil Lewis. If such an order was issued and obeyed the results would be horrendous to contemplate.

The concept of 'ownership' should be given serious regard. It should play a major part in arriving at the appropriate organisational solution for the particular institution concerned. Information can be gathered under the following headings —

1. Institutional: that which is genuinely the property of the institution and is perceived as such by the majority. The person charged with organising resources should have no problems from other interested parties in arriving at solutions for these items. On the other hand because they are recognised as belonging to the institution rather than to any particular department you will find (if you are just beginning to organise the resources) that such items have rarely if ever been maintained.
2. Departmental: those items which have been purchased out of the departmental grant/budget, and are seen as belonging to that department. Here 'ownership' may become more complex. This will depend upon the degree of autonomy given by the central power. Departments usually receive grants from the main institution and therefore there may be a need for some clarification of the official view of the status of equipment that is viewed as 'departmental'. This is essential if at a later stage decisions about the dispersal of equipment are to be taken which alter the status quo and therefore appear to interfere with departmental authority. Even if one envisages a situation in which no change will be made to the 'holding' of equipment it is still important that the record should show the 'ownership' of items of equipment, for from this one will be able to determine whether one has an equal right to use the equipment or whether one is making a request to an 'owner'.
3. Departmental by custom and practice: it is often the case that equipment is seen as belonging to a department because it has always been there. There may well be a sound reason for such practice — the tape recorders in the language departments, the typewriters in the commercial department — and these reasons may restrict the potential for those items to be loaned to others. However, decisions may have to be taken by those in authority as to the assigned 'ownership'. The fact that something has always been done in a certain way is no argument in itself against change. It may be, however, that the way of custom and practice is also the best organisational solution. Thus those tape recorders in the language department may be idle for long enough in the day for them to be considered for use by another department, but alternatively the fact that fifty working machines are required for each language group and that 10 per cent of stock are always under repair may mean that those particular machines should be for the exclusive use of the language department.

4. Individual: rare though this may be there are cases of staff providing learning aids which are their own property. Knowledge of this is crucial. It would rightly be considered offensive for a member of staff to receive a new schedule from the resource organiser detailing the redistribution of his personal property to another department. Where personal property is being used the following steps might be taken — replace it with institutional equipment; ignore that equipment when planning any reorganisation; or, by agreement with the owner, incorporate the equipment into the schedule under negotiated terms.
5. Outside bodies: the last category of 'ownership' certainly gives rise to the most problems. Schools may gain equipment through the efforts of a Parent-Teacher Association, in which case the owner is clearly the school. For further and higher education the sources of finance are more diverse. Grants are made by commercial and industrial firms, sums of money are left to particular departments (usually medical or veterinary) in family bequests, research grants are awarded by a host of bodies. Out of all of these audio-visual equipment may be bought. The difficulties of including this equipment in any listing is directly proportional to the number of conditions that were included in the original grant. It may be that, like the motion-picture camera on the microscope, the item in question was donated for a specific purpose. It is then difficult to alter the conditions of the original grant even though the function for which the equipment was first installed has long since ceased to be needed.

The main point to be drawn is that one should always check carefully on 'ownership' when listing the equipment that might be available. This will save embarrassment in the future and could lead to more efficacious planning.

What Uses Does the Equipment Have?

A simple questionnaire should reveal what the 'owners' of the equipment say are the uses to which an item is put. If any of the replies reveal eccentric use or non-use then this is another factor to be taken into consideration at the later stage of planning. The questionnaire should attempt to both quantify and qualify the use of equipment. Thus whilst one would expect the question 'How is your film projector used?' to receive the answer 'To show films' this would not be very revealing. However an idea of the number of films shown or the number of hours of running time per year could be valuable planning data. Knowledge of the university lecture room which was found to contain a 35 mm projector that had been used for a total of seventeen hours in five years led to a rescheduling of timetables to allow other departments to make use of this expensive and valuable equipment. The camera on the microscope could have been replaced with a much cheaper model which would have done the same job. This would have released an important resource into the production facility of a university — had it not been for the little brass plaque on the side indicating the bequest under which it had been received.

Data such as these, covering function, type of use and extent of use, are essential for any planning exercise. It leads not only to the supposedly cost effective argument which says that a teacher should lose his OHP and return to the chalk-board because he only uses it as a giant scribble pad and very infrequently at that, but also to the decision to leave the OHP where it is and offer some in-service training in its effective use.

What State of Repair Is the Equipment in?

A maintenance record will be an essential factor in any management of equipment. Any service keeps its credibility by being able to provide what it promises. If the provision of equipment is part of the service remit then that equipment must be in the best working order. At this stage of the exercise, in which we are simply concerned with the collection of information, the data on each item need not be complex; is it in working order? and if not what is broken or missing? Such a record will also indicate where equipment is being controlled and maintained by departmental support staff and at the same time will show where equipment is not receiving any regular attention.

In the longer term some regularised data collection on maintenance will be of obvious benefit whether equipment is centrally, departmentally or individually organised.

A note of caution must be sounded at this point. In seeking information on the hardware and the associated details listed above there will be an inevitable implication to many members of staff that somebody is trying to interfere with their territory. It is natural that in many cases teachers and lecturers feel possessive about equipment. This may be justified because of departmental expenditure or may be understandable because of the length of time equipment has been in a department.

ITEM:
MAKE:
DATE ACQUIRED:
LAMP NO:
BELT:

MODEL:
DATE DISPOSAL:
WATTS:
HEAT FILTER:

LOCATION:
SERIAL NO:
METHOD DISPOSAL:
VOLTAGE:
BRUSHES:

DATE		BORROWER	DATE		BORROWER
OUT	IN		OUT	IN	

Printed by Artigraf Printing Company, Buckhaven and published by the Scottish Educational Film Association, 16/17 Woodside Terrace, Glasgow G3 7XN. Price /100 on application. Approved by the Scottish Association of Educational Technology Advisers. Anyone copying this card is required to acknowledge authorship.

LAMPS		REPAIRS/MAINTENANCE		
DATE	INTLS	NATURE	DATE	INTLS

It is of paramount importance that this gathering of information should not be misconstrued by colleagues. Resentment towards the organisation of resources which becomes entrenched at this stage would be almost impossible to overcome at a later stage and could virtually negate any efforts to introduce the physical reorganisation of resources. Every effort should be made to enlist the support of all colleagues. If they can see that the objective of collecting information is to devise a system which works to the best advantage of the staff as a whole, if they can see that the exercise is supportive rather than intrusive, then the chances of co-operation and success are much greater.

Information about Incoming Materials

The survey cited earlier which was carried out in Scottish Colleges of Further Education showed that only a small proportion systematically listed materials that came into the institution. Since the survey, a larger number have taken up the notion. There appears to be nothing to indicate that the proportion of institutions who have implemented such a policy would be any greater if a similar survey were conducted across the UK, or any other country for that matter, in all the strata of further and higher education.

Learning materials are constantly being bought or hired, and new materials created in a variety of departments. Where there is a single central index of all materials, information on these incoming materials will eventually find its way into the index. What may not exist is a way of signalling to staff what materials have been newly purchased. A simple list of latest acquisitions can be issued if this is built into the system and is accepted as part of the job remit of either the library staff or the person responsible for processing the purchases. The reasons for issuing a list covering all departments are the same as those for having a single integrated catalogue — to break across the subject exclusivity of learning resources.

If the institution does not have any existing system for informing staff of incoming materials there are three main areas that might be considered. The first is that covering the purchase of commercially produced materials. A list, distributed at regular intervals appropriate to the amount of materials being bought (once a month would be quite adequate for most large institutions), would be of the greatest assistance if it contained the following elements:

Title of Item Physical Form Brief Description Where Held
e.g.
The Enzyme Game — Multi-Media Self Teaching Kit.
A game with tasks and work-sheets to teach basic knowledge of enzymes.
Bio-chemistry class library.

The second is a list of those non-commercial resources that are created within the institution. It is all too easy to lose valuable educational resources within a college or department. A member of staff may have many reasons for not wishing to make public material which he or she has created. There may be a natural modesty, or an insecurity over the quality of the resource. The act of declaring the completion of a teaching or learning aid may be seen as claiming for it some pedagogical or production excellence. The resource organiser will have to help colleagues appreciate that the listing of an item does not in itself imply any evaluation. The producer may be afraid that the acceptance of this public stance with regard to his work may invite criticism from other staff members. We must respect this anxiety and no one should be forced to declare in a public list those items in which they have no confidence. On the other hand, an open mind to constructive criticism is one way to improve one's own work. One cannot always demand a compassionate analysis and there are always those in any group who enjoy point-scoring and delivering destructive criticisms like poisoned darts. Perhaps we have to become sensitive pachyderms, aesthetic rhinoceroses, ignoring the barbs and responding to the good ideas. A further form of resistance often arises from the feeling that if others know about one's resources then they will be borrowed and not returned. The willingness to put information in public lists does imply a willingness to share a resource. If the item in question is required for regular use and its removal from the department would cause difficulties, then there is a clear case for the support services to assist with making additional copies if there is evidence of demand. The listing of such in-house materials would appear in the same format as the commercial material being bought in.

The third aspect of information on incoming materials is on those items which are only in the institution for a short period of time. These would normally be items which are hired or borrowed, such as films or video-tapes. It is not difficult to find situations in which departments do not know what films other departments are hiring or have hired. It can even happen between colleagues in the same department. Whatever the system used for booking films and video-tapes, whether by individual orders or through a central system, if there is some central point through which this information is channelled *in advance* then the following benefits can be gained:

(a) By issuing a weekly or monthly list of items that have *been booked*, colleagues can avoid booking the same film at different times.
(b) Knowing when films are coming into the building, items of interest can be previewed to assist in future selection.
(c) Unsatisfactory items can be identified and colleagues informed.
(d) Items found useful by one teacher can be signalled to other colleagues across departmental boundaries.

Whilst one would never suggest that a film or tape should be used for more screenings than the number for which it had been booked, knowledge that material is coming into the building can give rise to many savings. One of the greatest economies would be the chance to preview material which might later be selected or rejected. It will also serve to increase the awareness of film and video as a resource which should be regarded with the same currency as the book and can be as integral to the learning process.

Evaluative Data

It is not the purpose of this book to examine the various methods of evaluation within the learning process. That task is left to those qualified to do so and can be found elsewhere in this series (Knapper, 1979). Here I would take evaluation in a rather narrow and perhaps imprecise sense, that of placing some value on an item. If the information-gathering process that has been described so far is carried out in respect of the learning materials, there will be, in one form or another the following:

(a) A list or catalogue of the materials held within the institution.
(b) An indication of where these are to be found.
(c) A note on their availability.
(d) A list of materials created within the institution — which could well be integrated into (a), (b), and (c).
(e) A list issued periodically of incoming materials on hire or loan — which itself can begin to form a reference list of materials that have been used.

This list or these lists can let the searcher know what exists, where it is and how to get it. It may even indicate who ordered an item or hired it. The one thing it will not indicate is whether anybody found the item useful or not. It is dangerous to assume that because somebody uses a particular item every term at the same point in the syllabus, that it is the best for the purpose or even suitable. In the hurly-burly of teaching there is rarely a chance to give any detailed consideration to whether what we do or the media we use are in fact having the effect we desire. The periodic examinations based on information recall do little to examine the teaching/learning process. Faults may be more readily obvious in a skill-based course, or one designed for progression by mastery, but in the majority of circumstances the teacher uses his or her own judgement.

To have the media used in teaching fully evaluated and compared with alternatives might provide useful information. Such evaluation would however be enormously complex, requiring control groups and a host of factors to counteract variables such as the teacher's dyspepsia or the football results from the night before. Despite this it would be a great help to the person searching the files to know whether another colleague had found a particular item valuable.

The fact that a member of staff has found a particular filmstrip or media pack useful for a particular part of the teaching programme can shorten the search for another member of staff who is tackling an unfamiliar area. Staff leave for other jobs, some retire, some unfortunately die. Inevitably they take their experience with them. If a simple record can be made of their judgement of an item then at least that part of their contribution can be retained to help others. This can be entered on the lower half of the pro-forma document presented earlier (p. 66). In collecting these 'evaluations' negative assessments are as important as positive ones. It is valuable to know that, in spite of the attractive synopsis in the catalogue, that film is out of date/inaccurate/biased/ pitched at the wrong level for the students in question/too shallow/too deep, etc. Some of these judgements will be highly subjective but a knowledge of the person making the report can illuminate the degree of subjectivity.

It may appear that this is adding yet another enormous burden to the user of materials if they are to record their judgement of each item used. It may appear that it is imposing an even greater burden on the resource organiser and the librarian, but this is not necessarily so. As far as collecting the evaluation is concerned, the first time an item is used it should take only a few seconds to fill in the card. Subsequent

SCOTTISH CENTRE FOR EDUCATIONAL TECHNOLOGY Media Cataloguing Pro-forma	*Circle or underline appropriate sub headings*
SUBJECT AREAS	
TITLE SUB TITLE AUTHOR/CREATOR	SERIES
DISTRIBUTION COMPANY	PLACE YEAR
AVAILABLE FOR PREVIEW FROM	TERMS OF AVAILABILITY
MEDIUM INFORMATION	Single Unit/Multi Media Module IF MODULE, MEDIA INVOLVED (Ref. nos. only)
1. PRINT MATERIAL	Booklet/Worksheet/Information Sheets/Sheet music/Artwork posters/Photographs.
2. FILMSTRIP	Single frame/Double Frame. No. of frames b & w./colour.
3. OHP TRANSPARENCY	No. of frames Overlays/Masking. Size x b & w./Colour
4. SLIDE	Single frame/Double frame. No. in set Mount type. Size x b & w./colour.
5. FILM	Reel/Cassette/Loop. 8mm/Super 8mm/16mm/35mm Sound/Silent Optical/Magnetic Speed. x f.p.s. Playing time. b & w./colour.
6. VIDEO	Tape/Cassette. Tape width. Machine make/type
7. SOUND TAPE	Reel/Cassette/Cartridge. 2/4 Tracks. Mono/Stereo If Pulsed, System: Speed of recording/playback Playing time
8. SOUND DISC	Playing speed: Size Mono/Stereo/Quad If set, no. of sides: No. of tracks: Total playing time:
9. OTHER ITEMS	
SUMMARY OF CONTENTS	
TECHNICAL QUALITY	
SUGGESTED LEVEL(S) OF USE	Infant/Primary/Middle/J. Secondary/S. Secondary/Further Education.
EDUCATIONAL EVALUATION	
SUGGESTED AMENDMENTS/ ADDITIONS	
FURTHER RELEVANT MATERIAL	
ANY FURTHER COMMENTS.	
REPORT FILED BY	DATE

users need add nothing unless they strongly disagree with the first recorded opinion. A card can be circulated with the item or it can be completed at the point of issue and return. For disseminating the evaluation, if data on materials is issued as a list a column can be added so that the briefest of notes can be included, for example:

Item	*Medium*	*Location*	*Comment*
Oil	Game	Geology Dept.	Useful for 1st year revision (Head of Department)

If the information is held in a card file the evaluative comment can be added on the reverse of the card. (If typed upside down it can be read easily without removing the card from the file.)

Inter-Institutional Information

Data on commercially produced materials is readily available to each institution and patterns of demand will govern the way each college, polytechnic or university builds up its data base. Area centres might be considered where there are a number of institutions together, but this will require a commitment of finance and personnel on somebody's part. One day there *will* be a national data base of information on learning materials accessible by computer. Until that day we will have to rely on major information collections.

Data on institutionally produced materials is made available through catalogues such as HELPIS (Higher Education Learning Programmes Information Service), CELPIS (Colleges of Education Learning Programmes Information Service), and BUFC (British Universities Film Catalogue). That which can be retrieved through these catalogues is that which the producers are prepared to declare. Such catalogues can only be a partial survey of existing materials but they serve to illustrate that, however imperfectly, information can flow between institutions. It appears to require the effort and finance of bodies like CETUK to tackle the national distribution of such information, but sympathetic resource organisers can develop local networks of inter-institutional interchange

Co-operative groups of like bodies can, without too much effort, dispatch copies of their own software and hardware holding lists to each other. In the case of very large institutions with extensive collections of media it may well be impractical to exchange catalogues — in which case a person can be designated as the contact point in each institution. Such a person can phone his counterpart in the other library for information. In this way the questions can be refined, channelled and controlled.

Hardware data lists, when exchanged, can be stimuli to more developed work. The small unit which cannot afford, say, colour video editing equipment, may shape its production policy so that the need does not arise. When this unit finds out that there is equipment nearby which might under certain circumstances be borrowed, there is a good chance that attitudes and methods may change. There is evidence that several bodies changed their production and loan policies on the publication of 'Video in Scotland' (SCET, 1976).

Information Networks outside the Institution

In addition to the information that is contained within the catalogue collections described in the earlier sections, there is one final area which completes the basic structure of information that the resource organiser should strive to create. Book libraries are already part of a massive extra-institutional structure. The inter-library loan service that operates between universities is a clear example of the way in which an individual can tap massive resources. The public library down the road may be a small building but it is a doorway to a library system that spreads across the length and breadth of the country. Through the British Library Lending Service almost any published work can be retrieved.

What does not yet exist is any structure for assessing data on resources other than print. Taking any subject or department as a starting point it is possible to build up a network of useful sources. Most departments will have their own lists of contacts with other bodies. These will include other departments in nearby institutions, research bodies, professional organisations, trade and industrial groups and so on. The pattern will vary depending on the nature of the subject area being studied. Such lists of contacts may be highly organised but one suspects that in many cases the lists have been built up in an *ad hoc* fashion. It is also likely that these lists are idiosyncratic in that they consist of a collection of outside organisations that a particular member of staff has found useful in the past. Now, there is nothing wrong in working in this way, but as a system it contains weaknesses. If it is person-dependent, that is to say that a particular lecturer can get resources, advice and help from outside organisations because of his or her personal contacts, then the system breaks down as soon as that person leaves his teaching post. It would obviously be helpful to present and incoming staff if such knowledge were recorded in a more permanent way.

It is easy to assume that, because demands for outside help are being met, the most effective contacts have been made, and also that because one member of staff makes these contacts the rest of the staff in his department know of them as well. Both are somewhat dangerous assumptions.

What is being suggested here is that a more systematic approach should be taken to the listing of outside sources of information and resources. Because of the varied nature of such sources, and because they may range from the vast resources of an industrial giant to the personal knowledge of a particular individual, it is unlikely that the final collection of information will fit neatly into categories and be presentable on 5 × 3 inch library cards. However, it may be possible to stimulate a greater awareness of the range of resources that can be found within the community at large and thus persuade colleagues of the value of building up their own networks. For a small college it may be possible to conduct this exercise through the college as a unit, but in most cases it will be more profitable to do it by departments.

In 1978 an exercise was carried out for Scottish schools with the twofold aim of raising the awareness of teachers to the possible sources of information and materials and at the same time providing them with the beginnings of a framework into which they could build their own sets of addresses, thereby identifying a support network that existed outside the school. The chart on p. 70 was published, accompanied by a booklet giving brief notes on the items mentioned on the chart. For any FE or HE establishment the equivalent chart would look different but the principle should remain the same. One would expect to find more detail in the professional and specialist organisations; one would expect to find bodies such as the Industrial Training Boards. The differences that will inevitably appear between departmental lists are not in themselves important, the similarities are what count. For an index of these outside sources to become useful it will take time to build up, and so if departments can be persuaded of the usefulness of compiling their own indices of contacts then they must also be guided towards a realisation of the time it takes to create a record that will be useful to staff and students alike. It would probably be too much of an imposition to ask anyone to set about consciously creating this index. Rather than attempt to force the pace the resource organiser might first introduce the notion of the pyramid or network of sources and, once this has been grasped, suggest that staff members fill out a simple file card after any successful contact. In this way no one

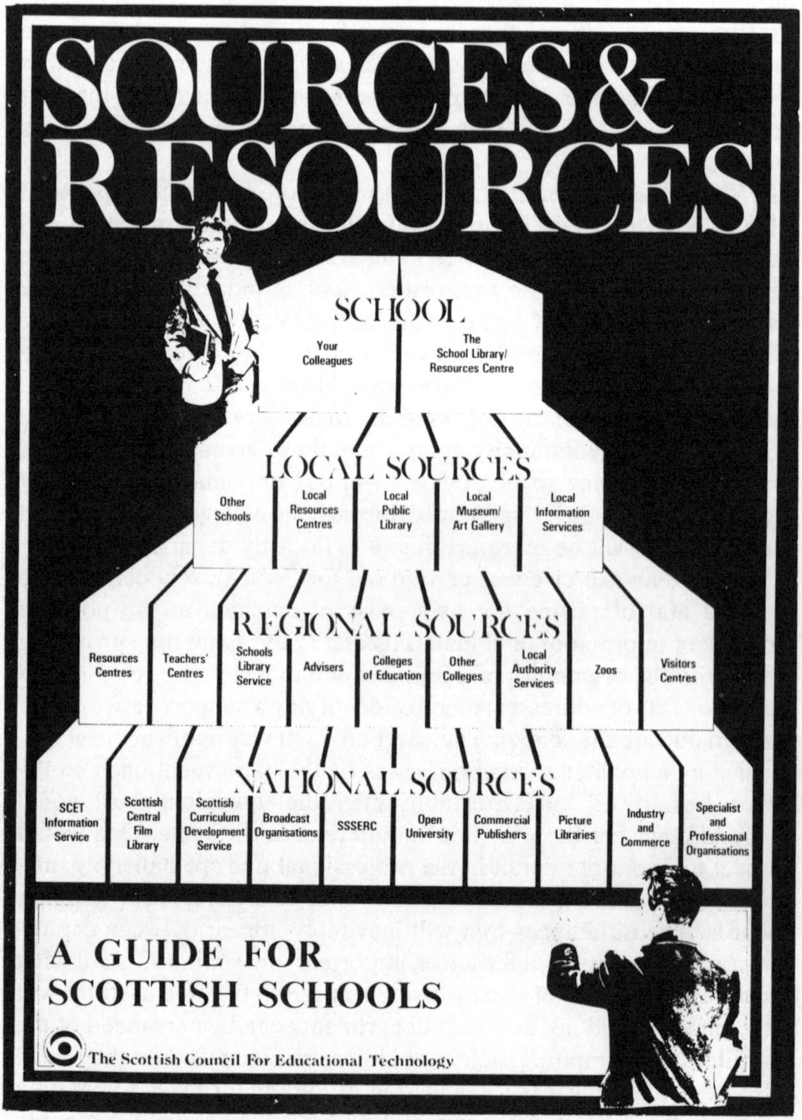
SOURCES & RESOURCES
SCHOOL
Your Colleagues
The School Library/ Resources Centre
LOCAL SOURCES
Other Schools
Local Resources Centres
Local Public Library
Local Museum/ Art Gallery
Local Information Services
REGIONAL SOURCES
Resources Centres
Teachers' Centres
Schools Library Service
Advisers
Colleges of Education
Other Colleges
Local Authority Services
Zoos
Visitors Centres
NATIONAL SOURCES
SCET Information Service
Scottish Central Film Library
Scottish Curriculum Development Service
Broadcast Organisations
SSSERC
Open University
Commercial Publishers
Picture Libraries
Industry and Commerce
Specialist and Professional Organisations
A GUIDE FOR SCOTTISH SCHOOLS
The Scottish Council For Educational Technology

member of staff will have more than a minute or two's duty at a time yet the collective departmental knowledge will gradually become a tool and a guide for future staff and students. The card can be as simple as:

Name of body..........	File Term
Address.............	
....	
Contact (Name of person contacted)	
Re (fill in here brief details of the information or service given).	

With the help of the librarian it should be no problem to generate a string of main file terms for any department. For example a chemistry department might have Industries (with perhaps some subdivisions), Professional, Chemical Research, Suppliers, etc. Cards can then be dropped into their alphabetical place in any section. The record will be imperfect but it will make the knowledge less person-dependent, it may drastically shorten the search time of the next person, and it may allow someone who is searching for one source to realise that there may be alternatives to the one first selected.

Networks take time to build but if a system is provided by the educational technologist which will allow people to compile their own, then the chances of the resulting network being highly relevant and meeting departmental needs are fairly good.

If all the preceding sections on information are followed through — and I am not underestimating the effort that it will require — then we will have the following as tools for decision-making and for direct learning:

(a) data on commercially available learning resources (software);
(b) data, or access to data, on audio-visual equipment (hardware);
(c) data on the software that is held within the institution and its location;
(d) data on the hardware that is held within the institution, its

location and state of repair;
(e) data on incoming materials;
(f) evaluative data on recently acquired or borrowed materials;
(g) data from other nearby or related institutions;
(h) data on sources of advice and resources related to the college or department.

Add these together and one has the tools whereby the resource organiser(s) can make the most effective judgements about organisational patterns. Staff and students can access appropriate information for their teaching and learning needs. None of this work is easy, and it will demand co-operation from many people. The skills of professional librarians will be required for the cataloguing and indexing of software. The whole process will take time to become effective but once it is in operation there is every chance that it will begin to affect the way in which people think; it may lead people to see that alternative resources exist from the ones that are habitually used, and a change of resources may lead to a consideration of a change in methodology.

As any librarian will tell you, if one wishes to create an information system that is easy to use there is a far greater need for detail and sophistication at the input stages than is ever apparent to the end user. Ease of output should be one of the main objectives of any information system, for if it is difficult to get answers the questioner will quickly give up and go back to what he is familiar with — thus negating the whole exercise.

5 ORGANISATION OF SUPPORT SERVICES

Having dealt at some length with the question of the organisation of information, let us now turn to the physical organisation of support services.

I do not intend to treat in much detail the organisation of non-book media libraries since many books have been written dealing with the technicalities of card systems versus fiche, key word systems and post-co-ordinate indexing. Nor can one offer any universal answers for hardware organisation. There are no 'absolutes' and solutions to organisational problems will, to a large extent, be determined by factors such as the physical geography of the building, budgetary constraints and staffing level. All that can be done here is to raise the issues which play a part in the process and point to some of the alternative patterns of organisation.

It would be a salutary exercise for the educational technologist working within, say, a college, to disregard for a moment the services that *do* exist and attempt to identify the support services that *ought* to exist in order to meet the needs of the staff and students. Having identified these, one should predict the work loads that can be expected with the present teaching methods and then allow for the increase that would be likely to follow once the services begin to alter the patterns of teaching and learning. Finally one should estimate the staff necessary to provide this range of services, together with the capital equipment and recurrent costs. Even by making wild guesses at these figures one is unlikely to have arrived anywhere near the levels found in reality. What one would have achieved is to have produced a set of goals towards which to work, yardsticks with which to measure one's progress, and the basis of a case for expansion of the present service provision.

Few people ever get the chance to plan the support service provision for a new college or university and where this does happen there are often massive financial and political constraints. One recent case where the planning of the support service for a college was closely geared to the planned strategy for teaching and learning was at the Dundee College of Education. The progress of the development has been well documented by CET and is worthy of careful study. Whether that particular exercise has been completely successful will, I suggest, only become clear in several years' time. The methodological changes implicit in the physical planning and provision will require a long period of assimilation. Whether anyone else will have such an opportunity for many years is also doubtful, but successful or not, the processes of identification of needs, selection of solutions and determination of the levels of provision at Dundee can be pointers towards ways of approaching the problems of organisation.

To return to the reality of one's own institution will in most cases be depressing and in all cases reveal short-falls from some ideal pattern. There will never be enough money, staff, space or time to provide an ideal service. Therefore the art of creating the best possible set of support services in any given circumstances is the art of making the most efficacious compromises.

The Organisation of Software

How does one effect the best organisation of software? This problem has to be tackled at two levels. First one has to consider the place or places within the building that the materials should be held, and then one has to consider the detailed control and organisation of the different media themselves.

For years the educational technologist has been wandering around like some modern Prince of Denmark muttering 'To centralise or not to centralise, that is the question.' One can take it for granted that whatever solution is arrived at, one will still have to bear the slings and arrows of outrageous fortune. Despite the rapid growth of resource centres there never have been any simple answers. In the final analysis the decisions on centralisation of resources or dispersed collections are taken as much because of the personalities of the people involved, their foibles and their political power, as they are on any objective assessment of the logistics of media storage and distribution.

If we recognise this and grant that the human element can and will distort any objective assessment, we can at least begin to examine some of the physical and managerial weight that we shall place on the balance trays of our scales of judgement. To begin with, if we have collected all the information about the resources into one place for the reasons outlined in the previous section, and if we have enlisted the full co-operation of professional librarians in this exercise, then there is the strongest possible case for bringing the media resources under the managerial control of the professional librarian in just the same way as we currently expect them to control books. Just as it was argued earlier that there is little point in trying to invent a new system for cataloguing 'non-books' because they are somehow different from books, there is also no intrinsic reason why the library should not hold and loan out 'non-books'. There may be additional requirements for storage, access and 'reading' as we shall see shortly. If we were operating in another language, such as French, in which book and non-book can be referred to by the same term 'document' we might not have created so many separations between the different forms of knowledge carriers.

A small college might be able to implement the central holding of software and yet maintain sufficiently easy access for both staff and students. The advantages are fairly clear. In the first place the direct correlation between the catalogue and the holding will allow for the most rapid and accurate retrieval of items. A dispersed collection related to a central catologue would necessitate a journey between the source of information, the catalogue, and the item itself. This may then have to be taken somewhere else to be 'read' in the sense of being viewed or listened to. The central holding can effect savings through the purchase of smaller numbers of certain basic items than might be necessary within a dispersed collection. Control — in the form of damage control and checking the return of all items of kits and packages — is also likely to be more effective in a central collection. If the purchase of new items is channelled through this central point unnecessary duplications can be avoided, and trends of use which are likely to indicate a heavy demand for certain items can be spotted in time to order up the necessary numbers of commercially available items. Add to these advantages the reduced number of items of equipment, essential to 'non-book media' libraries, that are required for a single central library instead of dispersed collections, and the case for a resource library integrated with the book library becomes very powerful.

The common error that permeates much of the discussion of resource centres/libraries, call them what you will, is the assumption that any one description is mutually exclusive of all others. A central resource library does not necessarily mean that *all* learning materials should or must be held there. Common sense dictates that materials used regularly by staff may be retained by them for teaching purposes. The only question here is whether to have duplicate sets of materials in the resource library if students are expected to use those materials as texts for direct learning or revision. Equally there may well be collections of resources that are so subject-specific that it makes sense to hold them in subject departments. An example would be something like major collections of language teaching tapes. A university like York University in Canada keeps its extensive collection of language tapes separate from the rest of the resources. The logic behind this decision is that they are tied to an independent learning system of dialaccess booths, so the tapes, which are never handled by the students, are housed alongside the master tape replay machinery.

When one comes to consider other subject-specific materials one begins to enter the area of decision between centralised or dispersed resources. If, for example, it is thought that the collection of biology materials is of interest only to biology students and so large that there is no point in putting the materials into the central collection, then one has to consider whether there are sufficient resources, staff and space to sustain an efficiently controlled operation within the biology department. If not, then it would still be better to share the benefits of a centralised service and accept the inconvenience of having to go to the resouce library rather than the department. Much of the individual study of learning materials will be done in a library or at home in any case, rather than in a department.

It would therefore appear that, aside from personal and political factors, one of the criteria (possibly the main criterion) for deciding whether to disperse a collection is whether the place to which a collection is dispersed can itself sustain an efficient control operation, and whether in so doing it is creating any benefits greater than those of the central collection. Very large institutions such as universities often have the precedent of departmental libraries with professional staff and can make a good case for separate collections, even taking into account the need for the greater equipment provision over the institution as a whole. This may appear to suggest that the decision-making process is easy. All one has to do is work out a 'break-point' at which a departmental collection becomes viable. In fact, such decisions can never be so facile, for each college, polytechnic or university will contain many variables which affect the process.

The physical geography of a building cannot be ignored. Split sites may force a decision to house a collection in one place or duplicate the organisation. Combined colleges or universities with departments scattered throughout a town or across a campus create their own problems. However in times of economic constraint (and there is another phrase we will be using for a long time like some verbal tic) the argument for consolidating resources into the main library collection still remains powerful. The realisation that ethical considerations may mean that certain collections such as those from medical faculties may have to be kept under limited access does not itself detract from the basic case. The most likely model for maximum efficiency would be one in which a central collection, under the control of the professional librarians, would be supplemented by such extra collections of learning materials as are dictated by ethics, geography or specialised conditions, all under the umbrella of a total resource organisation. Thus if a resource organiser is faced with the introduction of non-book materials into the institution the search for an organisational pattern must include information, materials and equipment. He should begin from the premiss that the centralised model tends to create efficiencies by the reduction of overheads and duplication, and then add variations to this basic model as indicated by institutional needs.

The second point to be considered, and one which affects the decisions of location to a certain extent, is that of the media themselves. Each of the media needs storage space — often with peculiar conditions. Many of them need equipment by which they can be 'read'. Assuming that the departmental use of materials can be coped with either by the equipment in that department or from some central source, we will concern ourselves with the needs of the individual user. Whether or not the institution has a policy of individualised learning the user of the resource library is at that time an individual user of materials. Keeping this in mind leads one to a number of suggestions for the equipment that a resource centre needs.

Experience of many and various resource centres tends to show that all too often decisions about equipment have been made on the criteria of classroom or lecture hall use. Equipment is then installed which is used by individuals. Add together all the FE and HE institutions with resource libraries and there must be vast amounts of redundant machine capacity. What need has the individual learner of a slide projector and a back projection screen when a simple hand-operated slide viewer is just as effective? A similar question was eventually asked by the staff at McMaster University, amply demonstrating the shift of thinking which results in savings. The biology department, operating a Keller Plan system, had designed and built cabinets containing a Kodak Carousel slide projector, a tape deck and headphones for use within carrels. Each unit cost $500 in the early 1970s. One day somebody bought, from the local dime store, a canvas bag, a slide viewer and a cassette replay deck. The students collected the learning packages from the library in the same way as before; put them in the bag and used the pack either in a carrel, or more likely at home. The total cost of the new package was $30. As far as the staff could tell there was no diminution in the learning. Not only were there great savings in equipment costs but the number of carrels required was reduced. Nobody stole the tape replay units — but perhaps all the Canadian students had better ones at home already. This example is quoted simply to demonstrate that there are other ways to approach the needs of the learner than those to which we are accustomed through classroom practice. Another example taken from a Canadian university was the fixing of cassette replay machines to the sides of armchairs in the library. These were used by students listening to pre-recorded lectures before proceeding to the worksheets or packs held in the library.

The table below indicates some of the needs for storage and equipment related to each of these media. The list of medium designators is taken from the LANCET cataloguing rules for non-book media. The new Anglo-American Cataloguing Rules (Part 2) are not available at the time of writing but it is unlikely that there will be any major changes in the list of media. Note that by 'open' or 'closed' access is meant the degree to which the library user would have access to the materials for the purpose of browsing. *Open access* would mean that the materials are available to all for viewing or scanning. *Closed access* means that the items remain under the control of the library staff until the client, having looked at the catalogue information, requests a particular item.

Medium Designator	Equipment Needed to 'Read'	Access	Storage
1 Art Original	None.	Must be able to see the items, therefore open access.	Sizes and frames will differ greatly. Vertical storage is required taking up considerable space.
2 Art Print	None.	Must be open access.	Normally on paper or card these will require vertical storage in such a way that they can be scanned.
3 Art Reproduction	None.	Must be open access.	As above.
4 Ciné Film (standard 8, super 8, 16 mm, 35 mm, etc.)	Film projector(s) or viewing tables for each of the gauges held.	Films cannot be easily scanned, therefore closed access.	Films must be stored in cans on edge. The shelves must be strong enough to take the

Medium Designator	Equipment	Access	Storage
			considerable weight.
5 Diorama	Normally none.	Because there are many component parts and much space would be required, suggest closed access.	Diorama are often very bulky yet delicate. They take up much shelf space and can gather dust unless covered. The component parts will have to be boxed and indexed.
6 EVR	EVR player plus a television set.	Because of the ease of replay this could be open access. Cost per copy may suggest closed access for security.	To be stored like ciné-film. Extremes of temperature and humidity should be avoided.
7 Film Loop (standard 8, super 8, 16 mm)	Film loop projector dependent upon the gauge of the film and the system of cassette.	Because of relative ease of use, could be on open access by the equipment.	Loop cassettes are usually boxed with the title information on one end and can be shelf-stored on edge like books, or stacked.
8 Filmstrip (single frame or double frame)	Needs only a simple viewer or a light box — even if linked to an audio tape.	Open access.	Usually found in plastic pots with title on top. Suggest the use of shallow-drawer filing cabinets with dividers creating squares for each filmstrip. Accession number on the pot and the space. If the filmstrip is accompanied by a booklet or tape it will need to be boxed or packed in some way and shelf-stored.
9 Flipchart	Table or easel.	Must be open access. All the	Some form of vertical or suspended

Medium Designator	Equipment	Access	Storage
		details have to be viewed.	file is required. The flipcharts must be capable of being 'flipped' either *in situ* or easily removed to a table or easel.
10 Game	Various items may be required, but for normal scanning in a library a table is usually adequate.	Normally closed access. Parts of games can be easily lost if on open access. Clients should be able to explore a game on request.	Games come in packages of various sizes. Normal shelf storage of boxes should be adequate with suspended filing in large filing cabinets for those that are produced in wallet or folder form.
11 Globe	None. Some require electrical power.	Closed access.	Because of the variety of sizes, shelving is difficult and space-consuming.
12 Kit (general)	Various; but for library use should not require any more than a light box, a tape replay and a table.	Closed access.	Various-sized boxes will require shelf storage. Usually will be stored flat.
13 Laboratory Kit	May require specialised laboratory equipment and therefore not easily scanned in a library.	Closed access.	Variety of boxes and packages. Because experimental equipment may be included care will be required in handling.
14 Microfiche	Microfiche reader.	Open access.	Store in file drawers in envelopes with numbers or titles clearly marked.
15 Microfilm	Microfilm reader.	Open access.	Usually on reels in boxes. These

Medium Designator	Equipment	Access	Storage
			can be stored flat or vertically on narrow shelving.
16 Micro-opaque	Micro-viewer.	Open access.	Presented as single cards or in sets, these are best stored in file drawers of appropriate size in envelopes clearly marked. In this way they can be returned accurately after use.
17 Microscope slide	Microscope.	Open access (not normally found in the general resource library).	Special cabinets with shallow drawers segmented to hold the slides are required. Microscope slides may be part of other kits.
18 Model	Usually none. Electrical power may be needed.	Closed access.	Sizes can vary greatly. Often models are delicate. Will require large amounts of shelf space of different heights.
19 Pack	Various, but should be covered by the basic minimum of light box and tape recorder.	Closed access.	Like the kit, packs can vary enormously. Usually they are boxed for shelf storage or in wallets for suspended filing.
20 Photograph	None.	Open access.	Sizes may vary. Could be placed in large albums or grouped in folders in vertical files.
21 Photomicrograph	Microscope or special micro-viewer.	Open access.	Like the other microforms photomicrographs are

Medium Designator	Equipment	Access	Storage
			best kept in protective envelopes in file drawers.
22 Picture	None.	Open access.	The 'picture' category covers anything that doesn't fit into the other graphics groups. Storage will be similar to the art or chart groups.
23 Portfolio	None.	Open access.	Can be kept in racks or in standard filing cabinets. Numbering will assist in keeping them in order.
24 Postcard	None.	Open access.	There are several methods of storage. They can be filed in envelopes like the other small card forms or mounted into albums which can be stored on shelves like other books.
26 Radiograph	Light box.	Open access.	These large plates should be protected by envelopes which can then be held in ordinary filing cabinets.
27 Relief Model	None.	Closed access.	Relief models, like ordinary models can vary in size and need special handling. They are expensive on shelf space.
28 Slide (various formats)	Viewer or light box.	Open access.	If open access is allowed then a variety of

Medium Designator	Equipment	Access	Storage
			methods are available. (a) Magazines — easy to store and keep slide sets in order, but are very expensive. (b) Boxes — cheap, easy to store, but slides have to be removed for viewing. (c) Special slotted boxes or drawers — keep slides in order but slides have to be removed individually to view. (d)Plastic transparent wallets — allow for rapid viewing, and easy to store in standard filing cabinets. (e) Where slides are accompanied by notes or tapes these can be boxed with the slides in plastic wallets or the combined kits placed in special wallets.
29 Sound Cylinder	Special and possibly antique equipment required for replay of cylinders.	Open access.	Cylinders are usually found in strong cylindrical boxes with the titles on the lid. Normally stored vertically in deep drawers.
30 Sound Disc	Record player (or turntable and amplifier) and headphones.	Open access.	Stored vertically on shelves or in racks.

Medium Designator	Equipment	Access	Storage
31 Sound Tape (a) Cassette	Cassette replay machine and head-phones.	Open access.	Unless part of a multimedia pack-age, tapes should be clearly labelled then stored verti-cally on narrow shelves or in any of the commer-cially produced plastic racks.
(b) Open Reel	Open reel tape recorder cap-able of taking the largest reel in the collection and with the appropriate range of speeds.	Open access.	Tapes should be kept in boxes and stored on edge on narrow shelves. Tapes should be run through every few months to pre-vent 'print-through'.
32 Sound Track Film (a) Magnetic	Special 16 mm or 35 mm track reader, or film viewing table.	Closed access.	Normally kept with the picture reels of 'un-married' films, these should be stored on reels in the same con-ditions as cinê-film.
(b) Optical	Special optical track reader or film viewing table.	Closed access.	
33 Specimen	Normally none.	Closed access.	Specimens can vary from rock samples and fos-sils to specimens preserved in jars. These obviously require special boxes, shelves and handling.

Medium Designator	Equipment	Access	Storage
34 Stereograph	Stereoscopic viewer. Old materials may require antique equipment. Proprietory systems such as Viewmaster require special viewers.	Open access.	Stereo photographs can be treated as photographs, the card discs on the American system have their own standard card envelopes which can be stored in small file drawers.
35 Study Print	None.	Open access.	Depending on size these can be stored in suspended files or in folders in filing cabinets.
36 Synchronised Presentation	If the packages have audible cues the simplest equipment can be used. Otherwise the packages will demand specific equipment usually taking the synchronisation from a pulse recorded on tape (see notes).	Open or closed access.	Though complex in use the packages need not be difficult to store. Usually such presentations are boxed or in plastic wallets.
37 Tape-Slide Presentation	This form of synchronised presentation may require specific equipment. For single projection the pulsing system is almost universally driven by a 1 KHz signal. Multiple projection is	Closed access.	Storage need not be complicated. The possible difficulty might be the separate storage of slide sets for multiple projection.

Medium Designator	Equipment	Access	Storage
	specific to particular systems.		
38 Teaching Machine Programme	These are equipment-dependent, the specific machine must be available for programmes to be viewed. Computer tapes will also be system-dependent.	Closed access.	The programmes may be in the form of paper or foil rolls. These can be stored in tubes on shelves. Computer tapes should be stored vertically in racks.
39 Technical Drawing	None.	Open access.	Store in suspended filing system as other graphics. Flat storage in chart drawers will make extraction and return difficult.
40 Transparency	Light box.	Open access.	Store either in boxes or grouped in deep suspended files in ordinary filing cabinets.
41 Video Disc	Video disc player and television monitor.	Open access.	Until these actually appear on the market we have no experience of any storage problems.
42 Video-Tape (a) Reel	Open-reel VTR dependent upon the gauge of the tape, the system by which it was recorded, and whether monochrome or colour.	Open access.	Tapes should be stored on edge in cases, in stores controlled for humidity and temperature. Tapes should be spooled through periodically to prevent 'print-through'.
(b) Cassette	Replay equipment plus a monitor will be	Open access.	Cassettes can readily be stored, like books, in their

Medium Designator	Equipment	Access	Storage
	required for whichever cassette system is stored (see notes).		cases on the shelves. Though less susceptible to changes than open-reel tapes they require a steady temperature and humidity.
43 Wallchart	None.	Open access.	Suspended filing for ease of viewing.

The foregoing table gives brief notes on the equipment which would be required by a resource library that stored all the media listed and assumed that clients wish or need to 'read' the materials. As can be seen, apart from a few exceptions very little equipment is actually required and very little special storage need be bought. The exceptions are as follows.

Graphic Materials. Art originals, art prints, art reproductions, flipcharts, photographs, pictures, posters, study prints and wall-charts — should, unless they are small enough to be put in folders or envelopes, be kept in one or other of the suspended file systems. These can be very easily made from metal frames with the paper sheets suspended by clips from bars laid across the top. Chart drawers cause endless trouble with retrieving and returning materials. Rolling up graphics work into neat tubes may make them easy to store but it makes them almost impossible to use.

EVR. It appears unlikely that we will see much more of this strange system-dependent material again. However other hybrids will no doubt appear on the market.

Slides. Because of the variety of formats there may appear to be a need for different viewers; however most slides can be mounted in 6 × 6 cm mounts and larger formats are easy enough to view on a light box. As to storage it is simply a matter of choice, although the viewing wallets do recommend themselves in that they can be so easily filed in the ordinary three or four-drawer filing cabinet. Remember to fix the cabinet to the floor — the drawers full of slides can be very heavy.

Synchronised and Tape-slide Presentations can present problems because of the different systems. Where possible it makes logistical sense to opt for one system for the whole institution. The library can then operate with a minimum of equipment. Where more complex presentations are held in stock it would be unfair to expect the library to allow a client to 'read' them casually. Special arrangements would have to be made with the audio-visual department.

Video-tape. At the time of writing there are about ten non-compatible cassette/cartridge video systems on sale in the UK market alone. There is obviously a need here for as much standardisation within an institution as possible. There should then be a minimal back-up of equipment to allow for the occasional use of the other major systems.

Magnetic Tapes. Audio, video and computer tapes should not be stored near any strong magnetic fields, including main power cables.

Thus, with these exceptions and acknowledging that items such as cine-films and computer tapes cannot be easily scanned there is a minimum level of equipment that will be needed.

To view. One can use a light box, cheaply made, for most individual or small group work. If enlarged viewing is considered really essential then there are cheap plastic rear-projection viewers on the market. They appear to be durable but are cheap enough to be easily replaced.

To hear. A simple replay tape machine with stethoscope headphone is quite adequate for the individual.

Thus if a library is setting up carrels for the study of non-book materials there should be one or two carrels which can cope with the complex systems such as video cassette or tape-slide, and the rest can be very simple indeed. It may be an idea to place a light box or panel near the store for transparent materials so that initial selection can be facilitated. If plans are being made, please remember that a sizeable proportion of the potential users are left-handed; the provision of left-handed carrels is much appreciated.

As to the storage equipment, there are many excellent tailor-made systems on the market. They are also expensive. The great majority of non-book media can be stored either on shelves, with which librarians are expert, or in standard issue filing cabinets which are still remarkably cheap and durable. Two main types are required, the deep drawer type for suspended files and those with two inch drawers for filmstrips, microscope slides, etc.

The Role of the Library in the Control of Software

The table of media on the preceeding pages has served to show that once consideration is given to the holding of media other than standard forms of printed materials, one can no longer neatly separate the questions of hardware and software. The assumption has been made so far that if any library is to hold non-book media then it will also meet its obligation, to some degree, to provide equipment by which the client can see or hear enough of the content to make choices. Whether the library is also going to provide the facility for study or whether the student, having scanned the materials to assess their suitability, then takes them elsewhere, is a decision that has to rest with the management of the institution. If the library, be it departmental or institutional, does provide this suitably equipped learning environment then its role within the overall learning context of the institution can be seen as:

(a) the first point to which the learner goes for information;
(b) the provider of information presented in such a way as to assist in, or even improve, the learner's search strategy;
(c) the direct or indirect provider of the learning resources;
(d) the place in which at least the first stages of each learning activity can take place.

Thus its role, through the strategy of efficient information and resource control, can be seen as central to the effective operation of educational technology.

The implication for the educational technologist is, as has been remarked upon earlier, the closest possible liaison with the professional staff that run the library and the teaching staff who decide upon the materials to be held. A direct support for the library staff will be required in the selection, installation and maintenance of equipment. The degree to which staff co-operate may be related to the efficiency of this support. Therefore if decisions are taken to control the learning resources in the way suggested, high priority must be given to this technical support. The ways in which the educational technologist can help in the creation of courses will be looked at later, but it is worth noting that though it is normal practice for librarians to give orientation courses to both staff and students in the use of the library there could be considerable psychological value in the creation of media-based introduction courses to the media library. This will bring together the skills of the educational technologist/media producer and the librarian in a common goal.

The Organisation of Hardware

When one comes to the audio-visual hardware, other than that which has already been described as being installed in the library, there are two main areas of concern; firstly the equipment which is installed in teaching spaces and secondly that which is loaned out from one or more places within the institution.

Fixed Installations

As far as the control of fixed equipment goes there is first of all the question of selection and correct installation and then the matter of establishing a regular maintenance schedule. It is amazing to hear the number of stories people tell about mistakes that have been made in the planning and installing of equipment. There is the slide projector that must be tilted down at such a steep angle in order to hit the screen that the mechanism can't handle the slides and the whole thing jams up. I personally have seen a projection port just under the ceiling of a room, high on the back wall, so that the top of the projection beam runs close to and parallel with the ceiling right to the screen. But the full humour of this arrangement does not become apparent until one goes into the projection box. It is on a mezzanine floor and the projector actually rests on the floor in order to get the beam out through the port; the projectionist must therefore lie on his stomach to project and see the screen. That is in a building completed in 1974. A brand-new school, opened in the autumn of 1978, has a projection box in its main hall which is so short from front to back that it is impossible to fit reels to an ordinary 16 mm projector inside it. A way was discovered to get round this, but the projectionist now has to go into the box first before the projector is rigged and cannot leave until the end of the show, as the door is on the wrong side. However none of this matters much because in any case the back two rows of the audience sit squarely in front of the projection window.

None of these are extreme examples; almost anyone who has been involved with the planning of audio-visual installations can give equally horrifying ones. Architects are easy targets for the brickbats and perhaps they should be able to spot such errors, but they rarely receive an adequate brief. It is often the case in new buildings that the educational technologist or the audio-visual specialist is not appointed, and certainly not consulted, until the building is complete. Whilst there is considerable documentation available on the planning and installation of equipment in learning spaces there is not yet an authoritative document which draws all the pieces together. At the time of writing a code of practice is being drafted for the British Standards Institute and it is to be hoped that its publication will not be far behind that of this book.

Without going into the details to be covered by the code of practice there are a number of basic principles that can be observed.

Is It the Right Machine for the Job? Find out what is expected of the machine; that is to say, not just what people will expect the machine to do when they switch it on but also what will be expected of it in six months' time when the users begin to think of additional things that they would like the equipment to do. For example there is little point in purchasing a hand-operated slide projector just because the member of staff putting in the request is more familiar with that type of equipment, if it is envisaged that there will be a need for combined tape-slide programmes driven by pulses recorded on the tape. Will the item be capable of being integrated into a more complex machine system at a later date if required? It is poor economics to have to jettison the existing equipment every time development of a system takes place. The process of making the decision on purchase of equipment need not be complicated. It does however require careful thought, an awareness of the 'state of the art' in any species of equipment, and the diplomatic questioning of the potential users.

Equipment which is to be placed in fixed installations such as that within lecture theatres and projection boxes is likely to last longer than equipment which is loaned out for use in classrooms, laboratories and other learning spaces. This is partly due to the fact that it is not being moved around as much, but also because in practice it tends to be operated by fewer people. If technicians are commonly used to operate projection box equipment then they are likely to treat that equipment with greater care than the lecturer who may feel no sense of personal responsibility for equipment that he uses infrequently. As a result one is purchasing equipment that must satisfy both known and predicted needs yet is likely to last for many years in use. There is a case for buying good quality, for in the long run the cost is to be amortised over a fairly long period, even if accountants write of capital expenditure at the end of the year. One therefore requires equipment which will last and yet give the consistent quality of performance that the staff and students can reasonably demand. The cheapest equipment is sometimes a false economy.

The other side of this particular coin is that there is sometimes a danger of selecting equipment with facilities which are never going to be used. At the stage of making the decisions about film projectors, for example, one has to decide whether there is ever going to be a need for the recording or playing back of magnetic sound tracks. It may be sufficient to have just one such machine in the institution which can be used when required. A great many film projectors are bought with the magnetic head as well as the optical head. If the number of machines on which there is a magnetic head which is never used is multiplied by the cost difference between the two types of projector, one can see that there is a large amount of money that could be saved — or used to buy other equipment. Similarly with the purchase of television sets for installation in lecture theatres the question might arise over the need for sets which will display an NTSC signal in addition to the usual PAL. Here one has to make an estimate of the number of tapes, recorded on NTSC, that might be received from North America or Japan. One facility for such replay within the building might be adequate. If this has not been thought of, then either equipment will have to be borrowed if it is necessary to view such a tape or an expensive exercise of standards conversion will have to be entered into.

Careful consideration of all these factors of present and future use will enable the resource organiser to select the correct items of equipment. It should be remembered in all cases that it is better to start from the learning/teaching objectives rather than from any vague ideas that a particular facility is required. 'Is your television really necessary?' (substitute any other item of equipment for the word 'television') is a question that should always be asked. If the answer is 'No', then don't purchase the equipment and demonstrate instead that there are other, more suitable means of communication. It is too easy to get caught in the status trap which leads to the purchase of high technology because other people have it.

Can the Output of the Equipment Be Seen/Heard Properly? Here we are entering more technical fields. If you do not have the necessary technical knowledge, the first thing to do is to consult those who have. A colleague may be a hi-fi buff and talk expansively about speaker outputs, impedances, tweeters and woofers, but unless you are prepared to stand by expensive purchases made on his judgement it is better to seek expert advice on the selection and installation of loudspeakers. Have the signal-generating machines such as amplifiers and tape recorders been carefully selected, matching the loudspeaker systems, so that sound can be replayed undistorted in the learning space when it is almost empty and when it is full? Do all the projectors produce enough light output to give an adequately bright image on the screen? Will an image hit the screen so that the axis of the beam is at 90° to the surface, thus avoiding distortion? If an image is to be viewed

— either a printed display, a projected image or a display on a cathode ray tube — is it large enough for the size of audience? Is the audience placed within the recommended angles of view and do they all have clear and uninterrupted sight lines?

These and many other similar questions should be asked by the person considering the installation of equipment. Many of the technical details are contained within standards documents issued by the British Standards Institute. As has already been stated a code of practice for the design of learning spaces and the installation of audio-visual equipment is being prepared by the BSI at the time of writing this book. Many other publications offer advice in this field, some of which are given in the bibliography.

The basic question that must be asked, however, is really very simple. When considering the installation of audio-visual equipment one should make sure that the visual material can be seen clearly, undistorted and without interruption, and that the audio material can be heard clearly, without distraction or interference.

The answers can sometimes be equally simple. Each particular set of circumstances will throw up its own particular questions. If within the framework of our present discussion of fixed installations one seeks the simple answer there are frequently low-cost solutions which can make dramatic differences to the teaching/learning process. A mathematics lecturer involved with technical drawing and measurement complained that despite preparing his isometric and gnomic projections with great care, as OHP transparencies they still appeared to be distorted when used in lectures. A quick check showed that all the screens in that particular building were of the type that rolled down in front of the blackboard. There was no way in which they could be tilted to eliminate distortion from the overhead projector. It was a relatively simple matter to fix a large board to the wall beside the blackboard, tilted and angled to the appropriate degree, and then mark the operating position of the projector on the surface of the bench. Painted a matt white, this board acted as an adequate and accurate screen. Other departments then followed suit; but it would have been more economical to have done this job as part of the planned installation, and as a single contract. This example, naive as it may appear, is quoted to illustrate the sort of problem that may arise if the initial questions have not been asked and to point out that solutions can often be low in cost and sophistication.

Can the Operator Get at the Equipment Easily and Quietly? Consideration must be given in the placing of fixed or even semi-permanent equipment to the ease with which it can be operated. Common sense dictates that there should be adequate space around each item of equipment for efficient and comfortable operation, yet one can often find cases where operators have to be gymnasts or contortionists to be able to reach round pillars or to operate equipment and see out of a viewing port several feet away at the same time. Can an operator move around without disturbing a class? Is there independent access to the projection room? If the equipment is within the same room can the operator work without disrupting or distracting the students — or the lecturer? Is it really necessary to have projection equipment in the middle of the seating area, or has inappropriate equipment been selected for that room? If there are television sets within a room can the controls be reached easily? If they are mounted high on the wall has any thought been given to providing a remote control panel so that technicians do not have to climb up ladders every time a set needs adjusting?

Here again the decisions that are made concerning the installation of equipment should take into account as many variations of operation as can be conceived of within that particular context. If the organiser puts himself or herself into the place of an operator many of the problems will become self-evident. When a draft plan of the installation has been drawn up it is a good idea to discuss the possible difficulties with some of those who may have to operate equipment. This will probably include the porters or janitors in a college or department, and their advice should be taken seriously. Many large industrial and commercial companies regularly put major problems before groups of apparently inexperienced people such as cleaners and drivers. The fact that they have not been trained to think in set modes within specialised areas often enables them to see a problem from a new perspective and ask those awkward but invaluable questions that begin 'Why not .... ?' These are the very questions to which the specialist has ready and negative answers.

If the Equipment Is to Be Used by the Lecturer/Demonstrator, Is It in the Right Place in Relation to Everything Else? Having put oneself in the place of the technician/operator it is then useful to consider the lecturer/demonstrator. Imagining that one has to perform professionally within the space into which equipment is being placed, what is the optimum grouping of equipment and controls for smooth operation? If one has provided the lecturer with remote controls for slide projectors, lights or any other equipment, are these placed in such a way that he or she is not standing in the projected beam? Is the microphone, if one is used, in the same place? Can the lecturer refer to the screen without having to turn round too far, or having to move too far away from the lectern? Is the OHP, if provided, on the same side of the screen as the rest of the controls? The questions can go on, but the principle they embody is that the final grouping should work to the maximum efficiency of the lecturer and reduce as far as possible those elements which can interfere with the presentation. We have all witnessed occasions in which a lecturer, having dimmed the lights, cannot read the lecture notes and has to run around like a character from a French farce because the equipment is spread out over several yards and the leads on the remote controls are too short. This may produce good theatre but it is counter-productive to learning; the students may treasure the image of the lecturer dashing around in the half-dark but are unlikely to remember what was being communicated.

Is the Equipment Safe? Now that Britain has the Health and Safety at Work Act of 1974, conformity with safety standards is imperative. Some audio-visual equipment, such as television sets, are covered by detailed standards as are most aspects of electrical installation, and there are standards that govern the safety of such things as stands for television sets and projectors. It is essential that those responsible within the institution are familiar with all the regulations and standards that cover their operations and equipment. Knowledge of the safety requirements as laid down can be important factors in the decision-making processes when fixed or mobile equipment installation is considered. Conformity with the standards may result in greater spending to purchase more robust or secure equipment and fittings, and although additional expenditure is no substitute for proper insurance cover it can substantially reduce the risk of calling upon that insurance.

It should be remembered that whatever the standards and regulations are at any one time they are only the base minimum levels from which to work. The code of practice to come from the BSI will contain pointers towards safety but it remains the duty of all concerned within education to ensure that every step is taken to reduce accidents. Cables between outlet sockets and equipment which cross in front of doors are obviously to be avoided and this is such a glaring error that one doubts whether it will often occur; however, a cable from any item of equipment presents the same danger. Where equipment is being installed every effort should be made to lead cables through the fixed furniture or carry them in conduits where they cannot be tripped over or damaged. Where a length of cable between equipment and socket cannot be avoided it should be taped to the floor for safety, or a walk-board placed over it. Such taping of cables is often cited but rarely practised. Over a year the cost of tape can mount up and the cleaners complain about the mess on the floor, but this is cheap compared to the damage and suffering that can be caused when somebody trips over an unguarded cable, pulls an unsecured television set from an unstable stand down on top of themselves, and in doing so rips the unclamped power cable out of the back of the set so that the already injured victim is electrocuted by the bare ends of the live wire — a complex but not unrealistic scenario. One college has already lost all its audio-visual support services pending an agreement on a code of safety practice, so concerned are the staff responsible.

How Is Maintenance to be Organised? The equipment considered in this section has been that which has a permanent or semi-permanent installation in learning spaces. This may or may not be under the control of a central unit or person. It makes sense for the decisions about this range of equipment to be under the control of the resource organiser for in this way economies and efficiencies can be achieved. Knowledge of what is installed where makes management easier. If the institution is new then standardisation can be introduced as far as is appropriate, and as a result spare machines can be moved to fill gaps left by breakdown and additional compatible facilities can be added where required. Spares can be stored in bulk giving a lower unit cost and a more rapid and effective repair service. If this main group of resources is 'owned' centrally rather than by departments, unused equipment can be redeployed for more effective use without having to fight the 'squirrel' instinct of departments.

If one is having to make a case for centralised management of the fixed equipment resources in an institution one has to recognise that the requirements of departments may differ as to the media which are most predominantly used. One also has to take into account the prevailing personal preferences of the teaching staff. Any suggestion that this central control removes departmental staff from the decision-making and selection processes will be deeply resented and is likely to result in a rejection of the facilities provided. It makes sense to have the fullest possible consultation over needs and to present clearly any constraints on departmental needs that may arise from the overall planning. Not only should this consultation be carried out but also efforts should be made by the resource organiser to make it obvious to those in a department that consultation is taking place and that they have a part to play in the process.

Whilst clear centralised control has its advantages there will undoubtedly be many circumstances in which a resource organiser is appointed when decisions have already been made and equipment installed by departments. Even if the departments can be persuaded of the value of centralised support there will be a period of several years before all the existing equipment is phased out and replaced. Despite this there is one service that can be provided in both cases, and that is the regular and effective maintenance of all equipment.

There are several reasons why this service should be provided if at all possible. If equipment is regularly serviced it will last longer and thereby save money. Regular service is likely to reduce the number of times that staff find equipment not working and thereby raise their confidence in using audio-visual aids. Even if equipment is within the control of departments it may be possible to persuade those concerned to join in the funding of central stocks of spare lamps, fuses, drive-belts and so on. In this way savings can be made over the institution as a whole, the departments get more for their money and they no longer have the burden of repairing their own machines. If through this system some standardisation of equipment is possible there may be the opportunity to build up a central bank of equipment which can be used to replace machines which have been removed for more extensive maintenance.

A well organised rota of equipment checking and first-line maintenance need not be as labour-intensive as might be imagined. Each item need not be checked more frequently than, say, once a month, and experience will show the optimum frequency. The use of the equipment record cards coupled with this service gives the organiser a powerful management tool. The essential element of this maintenance service, apart from being clearly cost-effective, is that it is an invaluable strategy for creating confidence in an educational technology approach. If staff have confidence in the equipment they are likely to be more sympathetic to the more complex and perhaps more threatening approaches of the educational technologist which are likely to have implications on methodology and practice.

Mobile Equipment

The second sector of the equipment field is that which, for want of any more descriptive term, we shall call mobile. By this is meant that equipment which is not considered to be so essential through its regular use that it is permanently installed in any teaching or learning space. In many colleges this group includes almost all the available equipment. Assuming that the audio-visual hardware is dispersed throughout the building there are a number of courses of action that can be taken to maximise the use of these available resources.

If, as was suggested in the previous chapter, information on the equipment has been gathered, one now knows where equipment is, its status or ownership, its level of use and its state of repair. With this knowledge one can judge whether to:-

(a) offer a maintenance service;
(b) service needs through grouped equipment;
(c) centralise and serve.

The Maintenance Service. As in the case of the fixed equipment a maintenance service for the mobile equipment has a number of benefits. From the viewpoint of the overall management it should ensure greater machine life and thereby greater value for money. It is a strong lever towards a degree of standardisation and could be the basis on which to build future development of the equipment policy of the institution.

The provision of maintenance is marginally more complex for the mobile equipment than it is for the fixed, the main difference being that if it is dispersed it is sometimes difficult to find. In this first case we are assuming no change to the organisation of the equipment, simply the provision of service. The obvious implication is that this is a labour-intensive exercise. The amount of technician time required will vary depending upon the number of items of equipment and the size and complexity of the institution – the judgement and experience of bodies who offer just this type of support vary so much that it does not seem reasonable to set up a rule of thumb that states:

(x equipment items) × (y departments) = p days technician's time.

It would appear that the best approach is first to secure the agreement of department heads for the principle of the support service. Depending upon the policy of the institution one may at this very first stage have to discuss the matter of finance. If a support service does not have adequate budget allowance of its own to operate a maintenance service then it may be necessary to charge departments for materials or for both materials and technician's time. Either way the service unit should be able to provide this 'first-aid' at less than the cost of an outside contractor or the employment (or diversion) of technicians within each department.

If the resource organiser/educational technologist does not have access to technical staff to do this job then it is worth investigating whether such a service can be offered, managed centrally but using spare capacity from existing support staff. In an institution of even a moderate size it would make economic sense to provide this maintenance as part of a technician's role. The cost benefit to the institution can be demonstrated in cases where equipment is not being maintained. Considering this function as only one of several that the person could undertake, it would not be unreasonable to ask for such a person if the increase in establishment is permissible. Another way of looking at the situation is in terms of 'savings detriment', i.e., how much potential saving will be lost if the service is not implemented. How long does it take in the break-down rate of equipment and the resulting loss of teaching before the costs have risen beyond the point at which a technician working for, say, one day a week is paid for? Each case will be different but all should be subjected to this type of scrutiny. If it is more efficacious not to provide a service then don't provide it, as long as the teaching staff who need equipment have access to an alternative source when their usual equipment breaks down.

The fault, however, with such an itinerant repair service is that it both takes more time than other more centralised models because the technician has to move around, and it also reveals the weakness of a dispersed equipment holding in that if the technician cannot find out where equipment is then it is going to be equally difficult for staff to do the same. In addition the technician has no way of knowing whether equipment will be required for use at the time when he wishes to have access for checking. On the other hand an advantage of this system could be that the record of equipment breakdowns would reveal not only the department that may be in need of in-service training but also the individual.

The drawbacks of servicing dispersed equipment point to other more centralised management patterns. At this point one must consider carefully the various forces that are at work in the process which result in the eventual distribution of equipment. It may be easy to produce models for consideration by the appropriate committee which demonstrate neat solutions to equipment management. Centralised stores may produce great cost savings and be secure and efficient, but the organiser or manager of equipment must always keep in the forefront of his thinking that neither the equipment itself nor any storage and distribution system is obtained for the benefit of the organiser. The primary users are the teachers and learners, and it is to their needs that the fullest consideration must be given. If at the same time one can demonstrate the economic and organisational benefits of one particular model, well and good, but there is no virtue in creating any system which makes it difficult for staff to get what they want when they want it.

Possible criteria for the selection of a model for any institution could include:

(a) an identification of that equipment which should remain in one teaching space because of specific requirements;
(b) the time estimated for the servicing of equipment and the staff available;
(c) the physical distribution of the departments to be served.

The questions to be asked then are:

(a) how can the staff achieve best access to equipment?
(b) how can this be balanced with the need for efficient maintenance?

One solution might be to group equipment around service nodes. These might well be departments or groups of departments. Here one could develop a series of sub-centres within an institution in which equipment that is required intermittently could be held, serviced and issued. Such a series of nodes could be supplied with spare parts from a central holding yet at the same time maintain a relatively short distance between the store and the customer. The staffing of such a system could be tackled in a number of ways. The equipment could be checked by a technican visiting each store in turn, the collection and return of equipment being the responsibility of teaching staff or departmental technicians/auxiliaries, though there is less security in this method and an ever-present risk of equipment not being returned or simply being stolen. Permanent staffing of the sub-centres would be one answer and would provide, for relatively small numbers of staff, an excellent service, but it is doubtful whether many institutions are sufficiently large to make such an arrangement cost-effective. The scale of some universities and polytechnics might make this pattern feasible, especially when the distances between departments and the difficulties of moving equipment from one to the other are taken into consideration.

Complete centralisation of equipment is an attractive solution to this service need and one which has been adopted by many colleges. Examples from the USA and Canada demonstrate that moderate-sized institutions, particularly those within a single complex of buildings, can obtain the maximum efficiency from the available resources by controlled central holding. Bearing in mind that we are concerned here with a relatively small proportion of the total institutional equipment and the fairly low level of demand by teaching staff for audio-visual equipment of this type, we can see that the consequences of central holding are not as fearsome as they might first appear.

Implicit in the concept of the central store is that staff *will* get the service they require. The service must therefore be able to deliver what it promises, so take care over the phrasing of the promises. If teaching staff accept that equipment will be removed from individual and haphazard 'ownership' and that in return they will receive what they need in good working order when they require it, then they must also accept that they will have to submit requests at a predetermined period in advance of the lesson. On the positive side such an order/delivery system means that staff can rely on equipment being in the right place at the right time, set up and ready to work. The equipment centre can manage the dispersal and retrieval of equipment on known requirements. They can plan maintenance schedules by building into the availability schedules the 'down-time' on any piece of hardware, and with good management ensure that the maximum use is being made of something close to the minimum acceptable amount of equipment. The disadvantages are that teaching staff have to identify their needs well in advance of a particular lesson and will not be in a position to respond to a question spontaneously by showing, say a slide sequence if they had not originally booked a slide projector (even supposing they have the slides ready). From the management standpoint the decision to centralise carries with it the need to have adequate staff to ensure an effective delivery system. However the time taken may be much less than is at first envisaged, as one technician with a large wheeled trolley can deliver and set up a considerable number of items of equipment in a very short space of time. If the system is established so that equipment is supplied for, say, a half-day at a time only three circuits per day are necessary, since collection and delivery can be made at the same time. If several staff are required for this job because of the demand then either the saving of capital equipment achieved should be set against these staff costs or one should reconsider the amount of 'fixed' equipment that should be installed.

Care will be needed to establish the best model for any one institution and there should be a recognition that the provision of an efficient service over a period of several years may change the pattern of equipment use to such an extent that the support model may need to be changed. For example it may be judged suitable to have a centralised distribution system to meet present demand, but a substantial increase in equipment usage may justify an increase in staff and the establishment of sub-centres. The need may eventually be felt to put all the equipment back in the classrooms, which is where we started. It has been said that a classroom is only properly equipped when all the equipment that the lecturer *might* need is permanently on hand. We do not have the finance for this utopia and therefore there may be a need to examine the potential of one of the storage/distribution models. For this each institution will make its own order form covering at least the following elements:

(a) WHO — is making the request (and on what date);
(b) WHAT — equipment is required;
(c) WHEN — is the equipment needed;
(d) WHERE — in which room is the lesson to be held;

to which one can add —

(e) SOFTWARE — who is to supply the software;
(f) STAFF — is any staff support required, e.g. a projectionist.

Having received this request the manager can then determine which machines and/or people are to be delivered and the order can be confirmed. If perchance it is not possible to fulfil the request then at least the lecturer knows well in advance and can make alternative arrangements.

Development of the Resource Centre and Resource Organisation

In the mid 1970s UNESCO conducted a series of research projects and workshops investigating the new role of resources in learning at school. Out of this work grew a report on the development of the resource centre. To overcome the difficulty of coping with the twenty different names that they had discovered to be in use in the English and French-speaking parts of the world, the term Media Centre/Centre

Multimedia was adopted to refer to what is commonly termed in Britain the Resource Centre.

Within the report one finds the following:

> The growing importance of informal education, the gradual disappearance of the notion of accepted truth, the vertiginous growth of knowledge and its increasingly scientific and technical character, are leading to the emergence of conditions which will enable the pupil's capacity for independent endeavour to be developed while he is still at school. Henceforth each individual will have, to a greater extent, to assume responsibility for his own instruction in the context of a lifelong education in which compulsory school attendance is no more than a stage.
>
> But existing school libraries or documentation centres are no longer fitted to meet needs other than those of already outdated patterns of instruction. From now on, under the combined impact of the development of the educational sciences and the advance of communication techniques, emphasis will have to be laid on learning and training. The organisation of school libraries and documentation centres should therefore be adapted so as to allow them to take account of the changes which have occurred in recent decades, both within the school and in the surrounding world.
>
> ... To sum up, the resources available — printed and non-printed materials — should be organised in such a way as to assist their utilisation and make it rational, *having regard to the new objectives.*

The italics are mine. A substitution of any other term from the realms of further and higher education for 'school' and 'pupil' will not alter the sense of this passage. If we are to take to heart the implications of what this means to the pupil in school then we have to be able to match the available facilities to the aspirations and expectations of those pupils when they move beyond the bounds of formal compulsory schooling. If we are to take the clear implications for the adult world which arise out of the social changes that are occurring round us, then we have to be able to provide resources and facilities for those who in the changing pattern of employment may elect to opt back into learning. The advent of micro-technology is only going to accelerate the progress towards recurrent education or 'education permanante' as outlined in the various reports produced by the member countries of

OECD during 1978.

If learning within the formal institutional course and through courses based on distance-learning methods or learning-by-appointment is to continue to move towards a more individualised base, then there will be an ever-increasing demand for the facilities offered by a media centre. The UNESCO report states:

> ... in order to convert a (school) library into a media centre it is necessary to:
> (a) reorganise the existing space,
> (b) redistribute the resources held,
> (c) remodel study premises.
>
> The space occupied by the media centre should be divided up as follows:
> (a) premises for small-group study and individual study;
> (b) facilities for the storage of teaching materials (printed or non-printed) which should be close to the premises reserved for study;
> (c) facilities for the storage and distribution of technical materials;
> (d) production workshops.
>
> The study premises should provide pupils with the means of consulting printed documentation, but also of seeing and listening to visual and sound documents.
>
> All these premises should be close to one another and be centrally located within the school.
>
> The various services of a media centre therefore require a great deal more space than that which is usually granted to traditional school libraries. The principal areas, set out diagrammatically on the next page, should therefore be designed and fitted out as shown on the next page.

This basic diagram can be marginally altered for the institutions under discussion here. The 'staff room' can be replaced by the administrative and librarians' accommodation. The main strength of the model, which is only descriptive of relationships, is that it demonstrates that the overlap between people, printed resources and audio-visual resources lies in the centralised indices.

The report then goes on to recommend two models for development from this theoretical relationship.

> Then, depending on requirements and available means, these premises can be supplemented by others as the need becomes apparent.

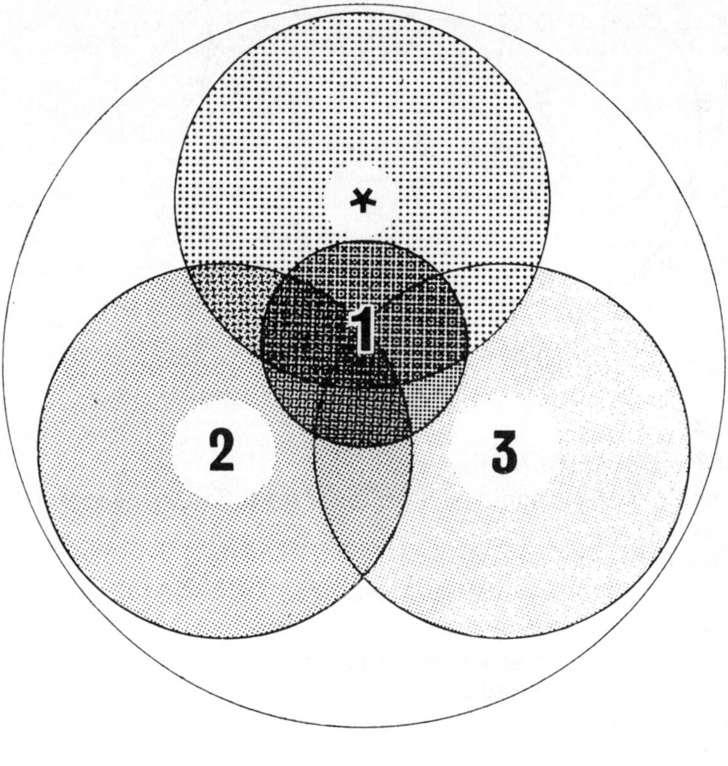

1. Card indexes - reference works.
2. Storage facilities for audio-visual materials.
3. Storage facilities for printed materials.

* Staff-room.

The following diagram shows all the facilities to be established and fitted up in so far as the range of possible choices permits.

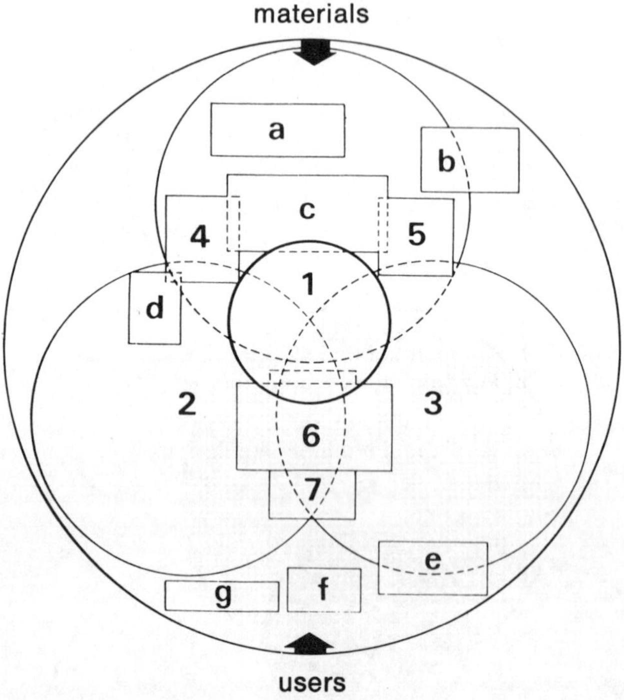

'BASIC' CENTRE (in figures)
All media centres should have areas for the following purposes available to users:
1 Card indexes, reference works
2 Storage of audio-visual materials
3 Storage of printed materials
4 Production of audio-visual materials
5 Production of printed materials
6 Group work
7 Individual work

'IDEAL'CENTRE (in letters)
If financial resources permit, areas for the following purposes can be added:
a Administration, management, reception

b Maintenance
c Office
d Distribution
e Rapid consultation and relaxation
f Exhibitions
g Lectures

The conversion will be effected in successive stages. The first step will be to organise those premises that are essential for the implementation of the strategies envisaged:

consultation room(s),
room(s) for group work and individual work,
card indexes,
storage of materials,
production areas.

This notional diagram has been found to provide the basis for an architectural development where the number of resources and users is small. In larger institutions the physical separation of elements may be forced upon those creating the resource centre, but this separation in itself does nothing to alter the relationships that are expressed in both the 'basic' and the 'ideal' plan.

It is not the purpose of this book to describe the layout of development of the resource centre. Many other authors have already done this and some are cited in the bibliography. Books on the establishment of the *school* resource centre are full of useful tips, particularly ways of storing and retrieving resources. If such centres can stand the heavy use that is made of them by small children, much can be learned from them by those serving clients who are at least bigger if not necessarily more mature. One can only recommend that anyone involved in the actual planning of a resource centre reads all that is available, particularly the case studies. The next stage is to visit centres that have been running for some time. It helps if you have worked out what your likely model will be within your own institution so that you can have specific aspects to observe in the work of others and can place what you observe in a context of your own. There is one other aspect of preparation that is advisable before visiting other centres. Be prepared to accept that the experience of others proves that you have been developing the wrong model. It is all too easy to set out on visits with an *idée fixe* and only see those aspects of other centres that substantiate your assumptions. Keep an open mind ready to listen to others when they describe what they did wrong, as the things that have *failed* in other models are more essential to your planning than a large proportion of the successful aspects. Most of the successful points are common sense and you do not need to be told about them by other people, but unless you ask you are unlikely to hear about the mistakes. If you repeat the mistakes in your own planning it can cost you dear. It is at that point that the person who could have advised you says, 'It's funny, but that went wrong when we did it that way. I could have warned you if I had known you were thinking of it.' So do not forget to ask about the things you are *not* shown on the 'visitors tour' of somebody else's centre.

The particular demands of your college or department will, together with the limitations of space, be the main criteria by which the resource centre is organised. The needs of the user must be the main criteria by which it operates.

The change from library to resource centre need not be major. Colleges of further education have demonstrated that the addition of a small number of simple carrels (even a large table with dividing boards between work areas) may be enough to engineer a change in the way that the library is used. This, together with a moderation of the staff timetable and the user access times, may be enough to allow for the development of learning-by-appointment. Such alternatives to the traditional pattern of enrolment for courses may even enable departments to maintain their staff quotas by playing the 'numbers game' with a new set of rules.

Whatever the physical planning of a resource centre and however it is related to the managerial and production services, there are a number of factors that any manager/planner should attempt to build in. As has been shown in the diagram, and as it is hoped this book has shown, the centre should have at its very core that which is at one and the same time the major tool of management and the main-spring of resource-based learning — the indices.

Next, every effort should be made in both the planning and the management to create a place to which people come willingly to learn. It is all too easy to fit in all the shelving, desks, equipment and resources and forget the user. In physical terms great care should be taken to make the place comfortable. If a student is expected to sit for extended periods in private study it is only reasonable that he should do this in some comfort. Hard chairs, unsuitable desk heights, inadequate light levels, poor temperature and ventilation control all serve to reduce rapidly the students' concentration. A place with too many hard surfaces will be 'brilliant', noisy and distracting, while an over-carpeted, sound-proofed room will be 'dead', pressing a blanket of unnatural silence devoid of any echoes on the ear of the learner. Add poor ventilation to the latter and stupor (over and above that normally credited to students) will rapidly ensue.

When engaged in mental work the human brain needs a relatively high level of oxygen and the eyes require appropriately high light levels; also, the human being responds to colours in predictable ways. It is therefore sensible to seek expert advice on furniture, light, air, noise levels, surfaces and acoustics if one is in the fortunate position of helping to plan or convert space for a resource centre.

If the centre is a comfortable place in which to study, if there is space in which people can relax and talk, then the first step has been made in encouraging the student to feel at home surrounded by resources for learning. The next step relies on the human aspects of management. Although long hours require complex staff duty rotas, the centre ought to be open to all for as long as possible and though controls are needed at both entry and exit, nothing should be done to discourage the user from entering. Even if a student simply wants to browse amongst the magazines or consult the catalogues in a random sort of way this should be encouraged, for it is when such interaction begins to take place between learner and resources that knowledge can be gained.

Control of Production and Reproduction

Within an institutional model of support services to staff and students one will find provision for the production of materials and some facilities for the reproduction of larger amounts of resources. Somewhere during the process of development there has been a recognition that if media are to be used in the process of teaching and learning then there will be occasions on which new materials will have to be produced to meet specific objectives. What is not always clear is what has happened between the recognition of this need and the installation of the facilities and the employment of specialised staff.

Analysis of costs and needs becomes very difficult once a facility exists and is in use. Demand tends to increase to absorb the whole capacity of any facility offered. For example a college without a professional graphics artist may find that from time to time the production of resources is below the desired standard because of a lack of access to good art work; but shortly after a graphic artist is brought on to the staff there is a rising tide of demand for art work that is now judged to be essential, so that the poor artist is trying to do the work of several people. Similarly the installation of a good plain paper copier suddenly reveals the need for large amounts of copying. In fact facilities tend to generate their own use.

We are not at this point concerned with the abuse of facilities. It is a simple matter for the organiser to check whether a machine or a person is being used for the most effective purpose. The graphic artist doing paste-up work for a non-essential job is a waste of salary; the copying of a paperback book for class use is both illegal and extraordinarily expensive. What is clear is that there should be a defined policy, made public and understood by the staff, as to what production and reproduction services will be provided and how they will be costed. One of the reasons for some of the apparent lunacies within institutions, such as the abuse of copying machines, is that jobs are rarely costed out properly. The Xerox is installed and the costs are absorbed within the institutional overheads. No one questions the lecturer who copies off the 75p booklet at a real cost of about £3 per copy. Questions may be asked as to the number of sheets used but nobody asks what has been copied, and nothing appears on that lecturer's departmental expenditure. Where costs *are* shown, they are usually simply 'above-the-line' costs, i.e., the costs of materials, items that are not covered by other institutional accounts such as staff wages. On the other hand, one reason for the abuse may be that it is very difficult for that lecturer to get money to buy extra copies of the booklets. Some institutions seem to make it very difficult indeed for small amounts of money to be spent, although it is often easy to waste large amounts.

There *are* many colleges or departments in which one can see that there has been a careful planning of the production and reproduction facilities. Where machines (and people) can be used in more than one mode (e.g. direct production and as a support for training) the facilities are so organised. What is most revealing about such departments is what is *not* there. This is often indicative of clear policy-making and analysis of needs. Whether setting out to establish a completely new production and reproduction service or re-examining existing services, it is useful to define the functions that can be undertaken by such a unit. The main functions might be seen as:

(a) The production of learning materials. Should the unit undertake the production of print, multimedia packages, modules, etc. which are designed as part of the students' course? If so what sort of numbers of each item will be required? What are the implications for staff and machinery? Can the machines chosen provide an adequate speed of turn-round to give a low unit cost?

(b) The production of teaching support materials. Should the unit provide for teaching staff those materials that they require in order to carry out their teaching programme? Can the unit cope with the production of a large number of 'one-off' items? Is a judgement to be made as to what will be produced for staff or will the unit simply act as a service for all its customers?

(c) Facilities for production of materials by others. As an alternative to the production of materials on demand should the unit provide staff members with training and, where necessary, equipment to enable staff to produce their own materials effectively? What would be the implications for staff in this offer of support through training?

(d) Facilities for student training. Should it be part of the function of this unit to provide training for students in the making of their own resources? This is of particular relevance to colleges of education. If the unit does have this responsibility what are the implications in terms of space, equipment, staff and disruption to the production schedules? Should this function be separated completely from the unit and if so what are the likely costs resulting from the duplication of equipment?

These are admittedly simplistic questions; institutional variations will exert different pressures on such support units. However even these questions demonstrate that there are several conflicting roles that can be thrust upon a unit. If the actual facilities and capabilities are not made clear to staff then the staff will place their own interpretations upon the production unit. Such interpretations rapidly become fixed perceptions in the minds of others, resulting in demands being made upon the service which cannot be satisfied, and the resulting rejection of the service will mean the loss of a valuable contact point for staff training and educational development.

It is therefore suggested that, if at all possible, broad decisions are taken on the *functions* that the unit will undertake before deciding upon the detail of the *facilities*. In doing this one has to take into account a realistic estimate of the finance that is likely to be available to the sort of institution in question. Grandiose plans for a studio with twenty graphic artists backed up by a huge print-shop would be out of place in a college with a hundred staff. The desired functions should be identified but not necessarily made an essential part of the initial plans.

Many college and university units have shown conclusively that most jobs can be done more cheaply by outside commercial companies than they can within a production unit, although this statement has to be treated with some caution. Costing practices were referred to earlier and it is the custom of only looking at 'above-the-line' costs that convinces people that, say, photographic work done in the college is cheaper than buying in freelance work which appears to be expensive. Careful scrutiny should be given to costings of this type. It may be cheaper to use outside firms many times rather than to employ staff and provide premises and equipment. Examples such as filmstrip duplication or film processing and printing are clear cases in which commercial firms can achieve a unit cost well below that of educational establishments because of the very high rate of through-put. Within the area of printing, the large commercial printer can produce work at a lower unit cost than virtually any institution where a large number of items is required.

What the planner has to do is judge whether to buy a facility when required or to establish a facility within the institution and retain a degree of control over the work being done, accepting that unit costs may be higher and efficiency lower. The facilities themselves can be divided into two sections; production and reproduction.

Production

Graphics. Look carefully at the type of work required. If there is a balance towards print rather than 'artwork', technical drawings rather than pictorial design, then select the right staff for the job. There have been many cases of disgruntled artists being forced to produce typographical layouts and page paste-ups; graphic artists, wishing to draw book covers, get frustrated drawing diagrams of internal combustion engines. Once the job is clearly envisaged the minimum staff requirement can be drawn up. Don't expect to cover all the aspects of the work, and don't ask any one graphics person to do this either. Be prepared to buy in freelance effort when it is required, and take professional advice on the equipment that may be needed. Most graphic studios have relatively unsophisticated equipment, but the purchase of items such as light tables and graphic enlargers may enable a wider range of work to be tackled by a minimum of staff.
Photographics. Clear decisions have to be made which establish the types of work to be tackled. For example, if the photographer or photographic unit is to produce both transparencies and monochrome

prints then this will begin to define the basic equipment required and the space to be allocated. Specialised requirements from particular departments such as medical photography, micro-photography or stroboscopic photography have been developed over many years and there is a wealth of expertise on which to call. Particular attention should be given to the thought that a photographer may also be asked to operate a cine-camera, or as part of the job to prepare the photographic plates for printing. Such added requirements could radically change a job description.

Type-Setting. Judgements based on the estimated volume of print production should lead to decisions on the level of sophistication. Electric typewriters, either automatic spacing or golf-ball machines, will be quite adequate for the preparation of much print work. In situations in which large numbers of different items are to be printed and good quality is essential, consideration should be given to word-processing and electronic type-setting. Specialist staff will be required to operate this facility and costs should be compared with outside agencies which do this job full-time.

Audio. For most audio recording within institutions the simplest of recording studios will suffice. Investment in good quality microphones, recorders and mixers should ensure better quality in subsequent copies. Where the audio production exists as part of a film or television unit greater sophistication of equipment is usually required.

Video. Video production can range from off-air recording and the simplest of portable equipment employing a single camera, to the most elaborate of multi-camera, multi-channel studios. It is not the purpose of this book to give any details of how such facilities might be set up, as there are ample books and journals devoted to the subject. The main questions to be asked should cover the *real* needs of the teachers and learners. A television service is a useful service to have but it can become an expensive way of writing on paper. If one can avoid the pressures of politics and status, one can operate with a low-level facility and borrow the sophistication when it is needed. This can safely be said from the knowledge that there is so much television equipment already installed in further and higher education establishments; once again the question should be 'Is your television really necessary?'

Film. Much the same can be said about film as has been said about video. Both are costly in terms of staff and equipment (and in the case of film, in terms of stock). Once a unit is established there is of course a great demand for the product, but with the plant that already exists one would have to examine the need for film and television production capability very carefully. If the institution or any part of it has a need for film or television as a recording tool (and there are many cases where this may be so) then one has to decide whether to give the facility to make 'raw' unedited material directly to that department in terms of equipment, whether to provide a service to shoot the 'raw' material, or whether to build up a facility which would enable that material to be turned into teaching aids. This latter solution is many times more expensive.

If film and television *are* judged to be essential elements within the chain of production then these should be incorporated to the appropriate degree. It is one of the features of planning that no matter what is decided upon, once the installation is complete it will be discovered that there is too little space in which to work, a great deal more storage is required and there are not enough work rooms. Anyone involved in the establishment of a film or television unit is urged to visit several units in comparable institutions (as well as in the show-piece universities, polytechnics and colleges). Ask the people running the unit to be honest about the mistakes that they made, the problems that they face and what they think has been forgotten. There are many good pointers to be picked up this way.

Reproduction

Almost every institution or department already has some capacity to reproduce learning materials, if only in the form of paper reproduction. As has been stated, even large production units such as that at the Open University cannot undercut commercial printers when the print-runs are in thousands, and therefore the prices offered by local printers should be kept in mind when planning one's own reprographic support. However, smaller units designed to produce high-speed output of relatively low numbers of materials have shown that in-house productions can be of a high quality yet cheap in terms of unit cost. The key to the success of such units appears to be in the careful selection of the correct machines for the job. In virtually all the cases of units that can maintain this low-cost/high-speed production, large sums have been invested in high quality, large scale, large capacity machines. The resulting efficiency often means that staff levels can be kept low without detriment to the product, yet at the same time high quality can be maintained.

Print. Most of the learning materials produced contain printed material to a greater or lesser degree. The charts (pp. 116-19) demonstrate that the different sorts of printing machine produce differing unit costs. From data such as this it will be possible to choose reprographic equipment — usually a combination of copiers and offset lithography presses with their associated plate makers and process cameras. For a typical establishment, see Clarke, 1978.

The various components of a printing system — vertical and horizontal cameras/enlargers, process cameras, plate makers, light tables, printing machines, guillotines, trucks/trolleys and storage racks — can all be related by the size of the basic unit to be handled. Although the initial capital costs are high, longer term economies can be made if it is possible to use A2 as the basic printing format rather than printing size-for-size on A4 as a standard. This will allow for several pages at a time to be printed at once. Savings can be made on photo-plates, printing plates and bulk supplies of paper. Linked to this would have to be a programmable guillotine to ensure accurate cutting.

Space then becomes an essential element of the planning. Whatever size paper is chosen as the basic there will need to be enough room between each of the machines for the bulk supplies of paper to be moved. In addition there will be need for space around each machine for stacks of paper going on to press and printed paper coming off. Without specialist technical advice it is easy to underestimate the amount of space required in the print-shop and thereby cause constriction of movement when the shop starts to work towards its calculated output.

If finance will allow it, it is advisable to install a collating/folding and stitching machine capable of coping with the largest jobs that are foreseen as being finished in-house. Though costly as capital equipment, the time saved by these machines — the enormous savings they make over hand collation, folding and binding — rapidly pay dividends in reduced unit cost. This remains true even if only a small part of the machine capacity is used for many of the jobs.

Slides and OHP Transparencies. Assuming that few institutions have sufficient through-put to justify the installation of mechanised automated slide copiers, very little extra equipment is required to cover all the likely demands for production and reproduction. Thermal copiers are cheap and often exist within the institution.

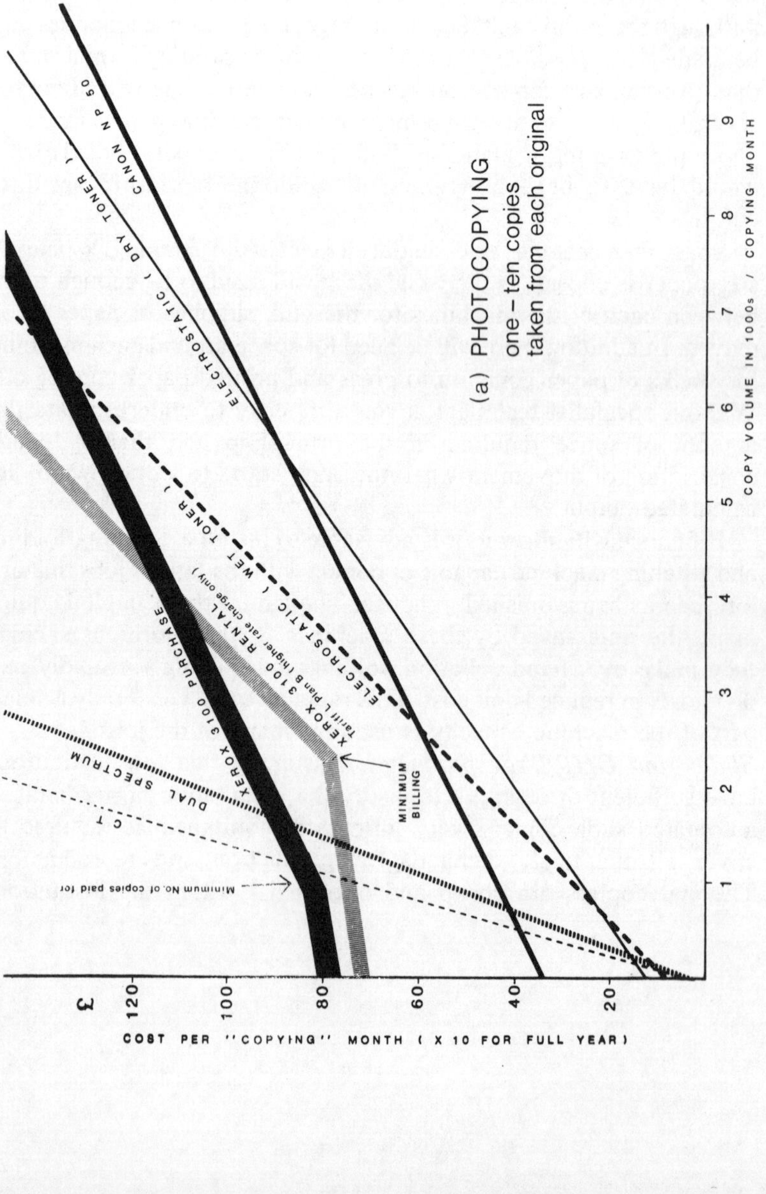
(a) PHOTOCOPYING
one – ten copies
taken from each original
CANON NP 50
ELECTROSTATIC (DRY TONER)
ELECTROSTATIC (WET TONER)
XEROX 3100 RENTAL
Tariff L Plan B (higher rate charge only)
XEROX 3100 PURCHASE
DUAL SPECTRUM
C T
Minimum No. of copies paid for
MINIMUM BILLING
COPY VOLUME IN 1000s / COPYING MONTH
COST PER "COPYING" MONTH (X 10 FOR FULL YEAR)
£

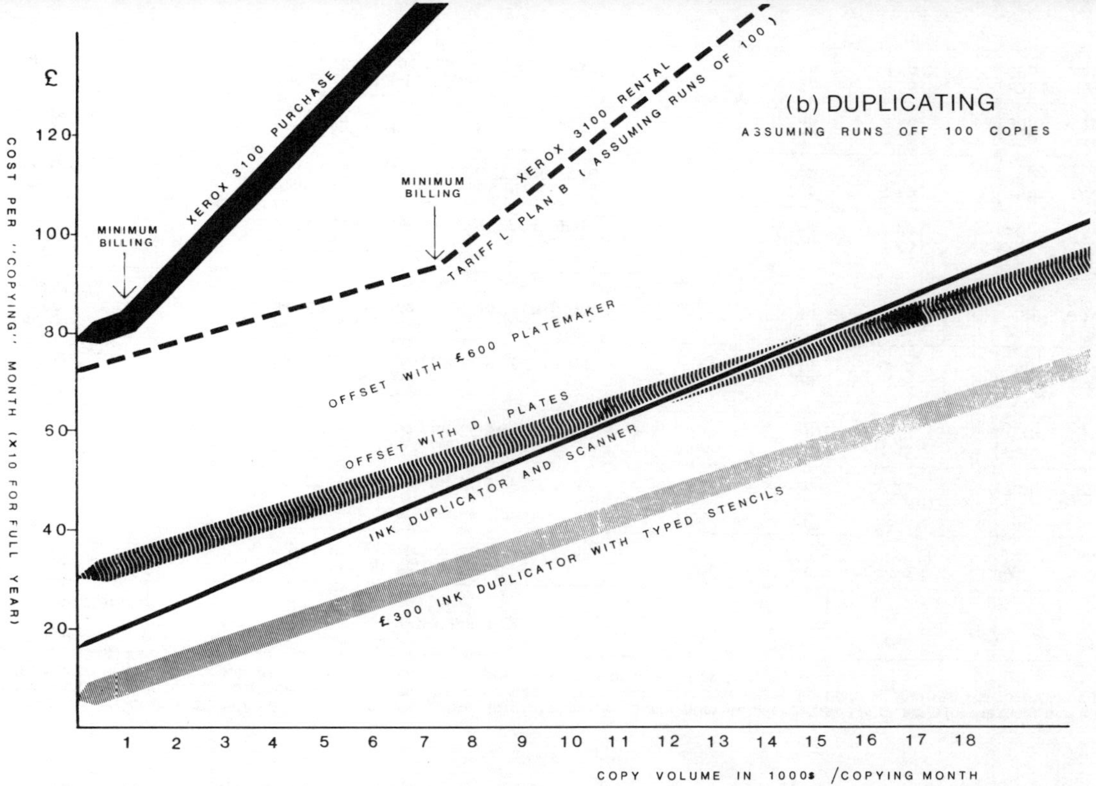

Note. These graphs are taken from the LASSET (Local Authority Support Services for Educational Technology) produced by the Council for Educational Technology for the United Kingdom. Though designed for Education Authority staff in Britain it is worthy of study by staff outside the primary and secondary sectors for the clear simplicity of its many good ideas.

Costs Per Copy for different lengths of copy run by different methods of copying

These costs are based on (a) material costs as shown above, (b) the real cost of labour (at minimum technician grade applicable for the task), and (c) an estimated time for the job based on reasonable practice. No allowance in these costings has been made for the capital cost of equipment or building charges. The costs of equipment used are listed in italics in the left column. The operator costs have been kept separate to point the value of 'free' labour!

Notional Cost of MACHINE(S)	COPY METHOD	1	10	ea	36	ea	100	ea
say £80	Dual Spectrum @ 5½p/copy say £2.20/hr. operator COST FOR TIME	5½p 2p	55p 20p	5½p 2p	£1.98 72p	5½p 2p	£5.50 £2.00	5½p 2p
say £400	Electrostatic (wet toner) @ 2p/copy say £2.20/hr. operator COST FOR TIME	2p 0.2p	20p 2p	2p 0.2p	72p 7.2p	2p 0.2p	£2.00 20p	2p 0.2p
say £625	Electrostatic (dry toner) @ 1.4p/copy say £2.20/hr. operator COST FOR TIME	1.4p 0.2p	14p 2p	1.4p 0.2p	50.4p 7.2p	1.4p 0.2p	£1.40 20p	1.4p 0.2p
(manual dup.) *spirit dup. £110* *thermal copier £120*	Spirit Duplicator and Thermal Spirit Master say £2.20/hr. operator COST FOR TIME		8p 4p	8p 0.4p	14p 5p	0.4p 0.14p	26p 6p	0.3p 0.06p
(manual dup.) *ink dup. £200* *thermal copier £120*	Ink Duplicator and Thermal Stencil say £2.20/hr. operator COST FOR TIME		16½p 4p	1.7p 0.4p	23p 5p	0.6p 0.14p	29p 6p	0.3p 0.06p
duplicator £200 *scanner £500*	Ink Duplicator and Scanner Line Stencil say £2.20/hr operator COST FOR TIME		16p 18p	1.6p 1.8p	21p 20p	0.6p 0.56p	34p 22p	0.3p 0.22p
offset £1500 *platemaker £600*	Offset and Static/Magnedry Plate say £2.80/hr. operator COST FOR TIME		11p 20p	1.1p 2p	16p 26p	0.4p 0.7p	29p 30p	0.3p 0.3p
offset £1500 *platemaker £600*	Offset and Paper CT Plate say £2.80/hr. operator COST FOR TIME		32p 34p	3.2p 3.4p	38p 38p	1p 1p	50p 42p	0.5p 0.4p
offset £1500 *platemaker £600*	Offset and Metal CT Plate say £2.80/hr. operator COST FOR TIME		62p 34p	6.2p 3.4p	67p 38p	1.9p 1p	80p 42p	0.8p 0.4p

Prices are as at 1 March 1978.

The costs on these tables are based on:-

(a) Materials costs (paper, ink, etc).

(b) Operator costs (based on the mid-point of the pay scale for the lowest grade of suitable operator for the machine — as shown earlier in this section — BUT calculated as an hourly rate (as in the Technical Services section) to show the real cost/hour (i.e. including such things as heating and lighting and support for the operator, and allowing that he is not productive for 100% of his time).

(c) An element for the cost of the machine. This is arrived at by setting a target for the machine in terms of copies per year. The purchase cost of the machine in terms of copies per year. The purchase cost of the machine is spread over five years. So one fifth of the purchase price divided by the target copy volume gives the machine cost element. If the target cost for a machine is 2,000 copies/year and the machine costs £200 then the machine cost element added in per copy is

$$£\frac{200}{5 \times 2000} = 2p$$

METHOD	36 A4 Copies Total Cost	36 A4 Copies Cost/ Side	100 A4 Copies Total Cost	100 A4 Copies Cost/ Side
Dual Spectrum assuming say 2000 copies/year	£2.99	8p	£8.30	8p
Electrostatic (wet toner) assuming say 10,000 copies/year	£1.08	3p	£3.00	3p
Electrostatic (dry toner) assuming say 10,000 copies/year	£1.03	3p	£2.85	3p
Spirit Duplicator & Heat Copier assuming say 20,000 copies/year	£0.27	less than 1p	£0.55	½p
Ink Duplicator & Heat Copier assuming say 100,000 copies/year	£0.30	less than 1p	£0.41	less than ½p
Ink Duplicator & Electronic Stencil Cutter, assuming say 100,000 copies/year	£0.46	just over 1p	£0.70	less than 1p
Offset Litho with £600 Platemaker assuming say copies/year 100,000	£0.57	1½p	£1.01	1p
500,000	£0.45	just over 1p	£0.67	just over ½p
1,000,000	£0.44	just over 1p	£0.63	just over ½p

Electrostatic copiers and the facilities of the print-shop can be utilised during the process of reproduction. Add a diazo processor to the darkroom facilties and almost any type of slide or transparency can be produced.

By starting with the envisaged needs the following sort of algorithm will enable planners to select appropriate machinery. The chart on p. 121 was devised by J.F. Murray, for a situation which had a process camera, rapidoprint, developing tanks and access to an illumitran. It demonstrated the need for a diazo printer. A similar process could be recommended for decision-making in other equipment fields. The main virtue of such an analytical approach is that the choices for equipment and production methods are derived from the desired outcomes.

Audio. As far as audio copying is concerned the equipment and space can be minimal. Such is the nature of audio recording that high-speed duplication on reel or cassette can be installed, at relatively low cost, to service the demands of very large institutions; but the decision to do this should follow from the known need for multiple tape copies as part of the selected learning method.

Video. Multiple reproduction of video tape is a more complex matter since for most formats high-speed copying is not possible and the special equipment required for real-time multiple copying is very expensive. This may lead towards the provision of either library copies of tapes or the installation of a central distribution system, thus satisfying a larger audience by feeding the signal to a group of viewers or by allowing individual access through a system of distribution to carrels.

Packaging. An essential element of the reproduction service is that section in which the various parts of multimedia packages are brought together for final collation, packaging and distribution. Whether each job is taken to its final stage or whether the consitituent parts for a package are kept separate until called for, there will still be a need for space, shelving, a retrieval system and people to carry out the work.

All that has been done in listing the elements of a service in this way has been to name the major parts of a whole. The way that they are fitted together and the detailed make-up of any section will vary so much from institution to institution that it would be foolhardy to attempt to be descriptive and dangerously misleading to attempt to be prescriptive. All that can be said is that before seeking professional advice about each individual sector make sure that you have a clear idea of the services that will and will not be offered, try to estimate the

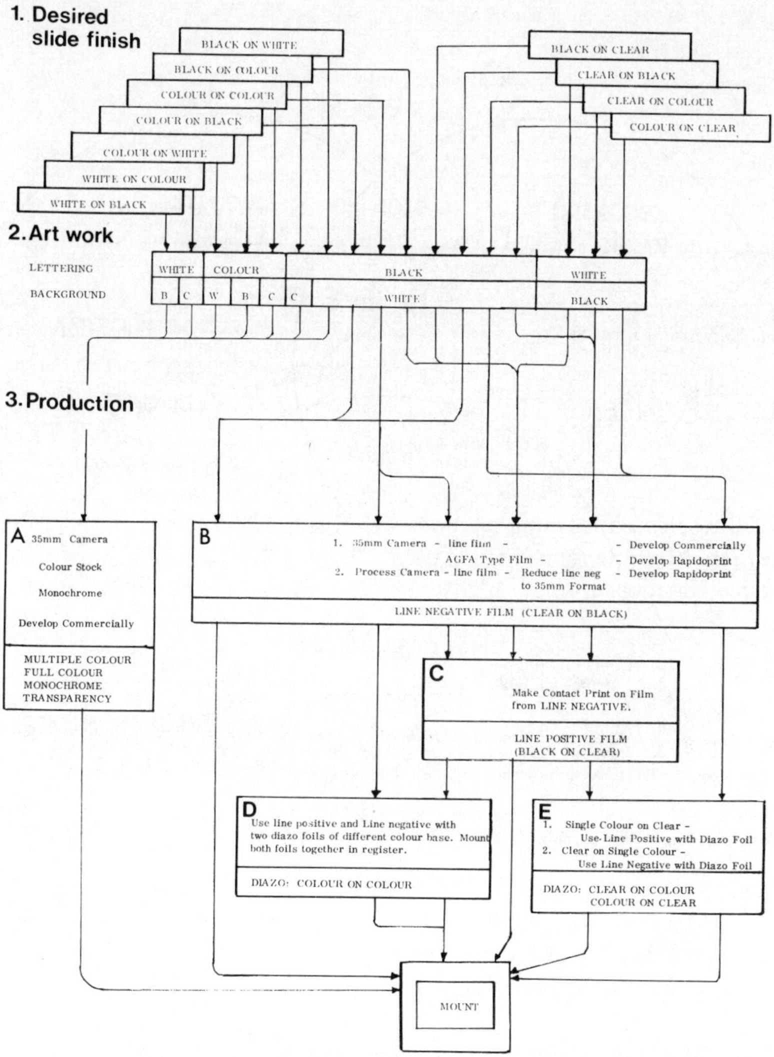
1. Desired slide finish
BLACK ON WHITE
BLACK ON COLOUR
COLOUR ON COLOUR
COLOUR ON BLACK
COLOUR ON WHITE
WHITE ON COLOUR
WHITE ON BLACK
BLACK ON CLEAR
CLEAR ON BLACK
CLEAR ON COLOUR
COLOUR ON CLEAR
2. Art work
LETTERING
BACKGROUND
WHITE
COLOUR
BLACK
WHITE
B C W B C C
WHITE
BLACK
3. Production
A 35mm Camera
Colour Stock
Monochrome
Develop Commercially
MULTIPLE COLOUR
FULL COLOUR
MONOCHROME
TRANSPARENCY
B
1. 35mm Camera - line film - - Develop Commercially
AGFA Type Film - - Develop Rapidoprint
2. Process Camera - line film - Reduce line neg to 35mm Format - Develop Rapidoprint
LINE NEGATIVE FILM (CLEAR ON BLACK)
C
Make Contact Print on Film from LINE NEGATIVE.
LINE POSITIVE FILM (BLACK ON CLEAR)
D
Use line positive and Line negative with two diazo foils of different colour base. Mount both foils together in register.
DIAZO: COLOUR ON COLOUR
E
1. Single Colour on Clear - Use Line Positive with Diazo Foil
2. Clear on Single Colour - Use Line Negative with Diazo Foil
DIAZO: CLEAR ON COLOUR
COLOUR ON CLEAR
MOUNT

The Relationship of the Elements in the Production and Reproduction Service.

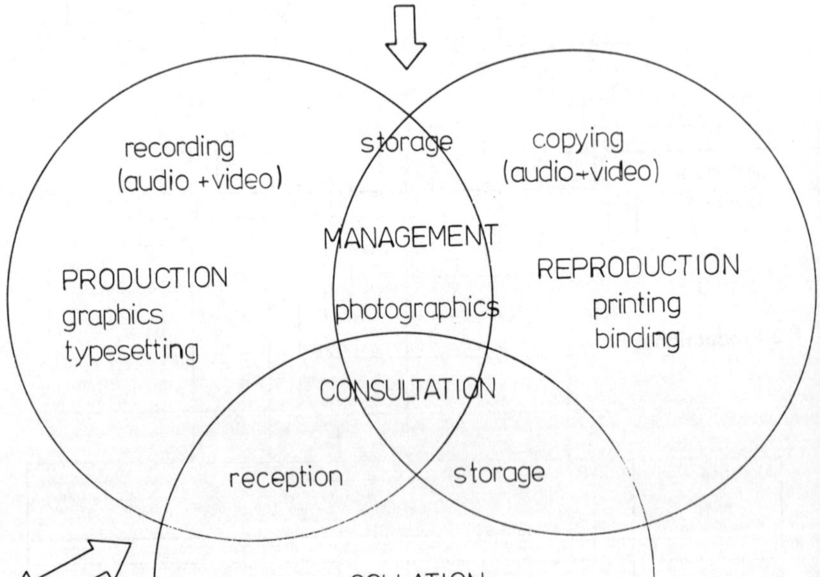

The elements within the production and reproduction service can be viewed as being related in the above way. As can be seen, the consultancy role, backed by the central management, provides a control on both the input and output of the unit.

The possible flow lines can be seen in the next figure showing that materials can move from one section to another through a series of consultation, evaluation, quality checking.

types and volumes of media that are and will be required — and then allow a very large element of extra capacity for the inevitable increase in demand for the services.

The Possible Flow Patterns through the Service

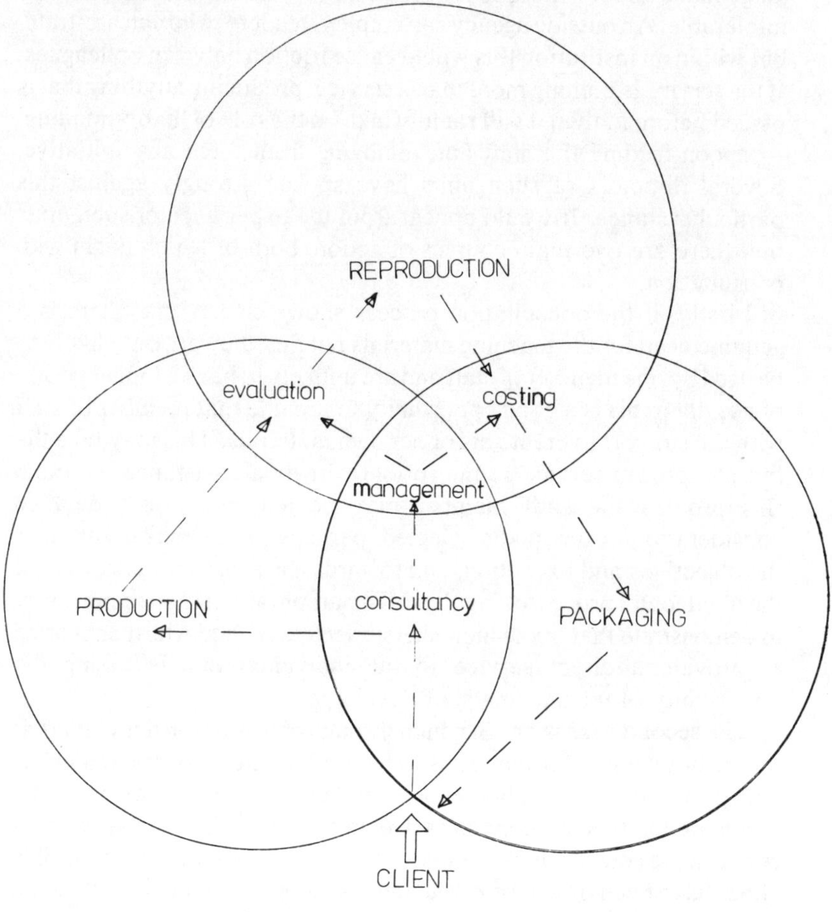

*   *   *   *

So far this section has dealt with the production service simply as a facility. In operation the resource organiser will be faced with the need to make decisions about which materials are to be produced, for it is safe to say that there will be times when the demand is greater than the capacity. There will also be times when the production of material is requested, or material is presented for reproduction, the quality and educational value of which has to be questioned. Standards will have to be set, not simply of excellence in terms of graphic quality but also in educational terms, by which priorities can be assigned. A system of evaluation of materials will be required, but for the resource organiser/ educational technologist to be placed in a position of having to make judgements about which job is accepted and which is refused would be intolerable. An outside agency can employ 'readers' who can arbitrate, but within an institution this would cause friction between colleagues. If the service is nothing more than a service, producing anything that is placed before it, then it will rapidly take on the role of 'baby-minding' — spoon-feeding the staff and removing from them any initiative. Several directors of such units have spoken strongly against this particular stance. It would appear from the experience of such units that there are two main courses of action, both of which begin with consultation.

Firstly, if the consultation process shows clearly that there is a genuine need for the teaching materials but that they are only likely to be used by one member of staff and are unlikely to have a longer period of use, then this is a good opportunity to provide that member of staff with the support to create his or her own materials. This may take the form of some in-service training prior to practical assistance. Through this process the staff member may be led to a more detailed consideration of the media selected, perhaps to a reconsideration of the objectives and execution, and towards a greater understanding of the intellectual processes involved. To paraphrase, it is an opportunity to demonstrate that 'mediation alters orientation', and whilst appearing to provide a direct service to the individual one is taking the opportunity of introducing staff development.

The second case is one in which through consultation it is clear that the requirement is for materials to be used by the students, materials with more than an ephemeral existence. If the service is to be committed to this more major task then there should be an agreement between the educational technologist and the 'client' that the materials either have been or will be evaluated, as there is no point in producing ineffective learning materials. If the staff member can produce evidence of evaluation then it should be easy to agree on the next steps, whereas if no evaluation has been done but the proposal still appears to be sound, an agreement can be reached as to an evaluation exercise after the initial production stages and before the large-scale reproduction. If the staff member has not thought of evaluation or does not know how to proceed, the educational technologist can either co-operate in this exercise or bring together the appropriate colleagues to carry it out. In either case the opportunity for educational development has presented itself, growing organically out of declared practical requirements. Under these circumstances and by this strategy development is more likely to be assimilated, the service will be able to concentrate on those items which have a recognised educational value, and the notion of staff development will have been introduced without any sense of threat or any implication of deficit.

In summarising the sections of this chapter we can see that by providing the organisational structure into which elements can be fitted, more than one purpose can be achieved.

1. Organising software storage and access	Provides ready access to resources	Potentially alters learning strategy
2. Organising hardware: (a) In the resource centre/library	Turns access into activity	Teaches method through practice — covert educational development
(b) As fixed installations	Provides a reliable service	Encourages use of media through the build-up of confidence
(c) As mobile equipment	Provides a reliable service	Opens the door to in-service training and staff development
3. Development of the resource centre or resource organisation	Builds up a firm base for activity	Brings together professional interests; could be one spring-board to further educational development
4. Organising the production and reproduction service	Provides a direct responsive service to recognised needs	Linked to all the above services this provides one of the best bargaining points in the process of educational development

6 STRATEGIES FOR ENSURING THE ACCEPTANCE OF THE EDUCATIONAL TECHNOLOGY SERVICES

The inclusion of the term 'services' is deliberate. Acceptance of the services — even if they are simply regarded as 'aids' — carries with it many implications for the methods and intellectual processes of the staff. Therefore one is suggesting that if one can devise strategies for getting people to accept, and get involved in using, the service aspects of educational technology together with all its potential implications, then this in itself is a major strategy in the process of assimilation of the broader educational technology processes within the institution.

It is obvious to me at this point that there are those within the broad compass of 'educational technology' who will react violently to the whole notion of providing *service*. 'Never be a service,' cried one of the best service providers that I know, 'always be a customer.' I am still trying to work that one out! There is however a good point made by those who reject the service role. If the educational technologist and his/her unit is perceived as doing nothing more than providing a service on demand, then the longer this goes on the more difficult it will be to break out of the mould; and if that is all the unit does they could be replaced by robots. The fault lies not in the approach but in the personalities operating the service.

There may also be readers who, if they have read this far, may reject totally the notion that anything that has been discussed so far has anything at all to do with themselves as educational technologists. It is unfortunate that the world is divided into two types of people — those that the divide the world into two types of people and those that don't. All too often the world is seen as being made up of stark black and white, lumps of mutually exclusive options. If we can recognise that we are all on a spectrum full of delicate shadings then the educational technologist who sees his function as, say, evaluation, will have to be evaluating *something* in practice. That something may be transactional analysis but even the forms for recording the analysis have an influence on the procedure; they are designed and produced by somebody. Even at the most extreme edges of educational technology we are all tied together and most of those threads are woven through the service element. If we refer back to the staff lists from the further education colleges cited earlier in the book we can envisage these people in circumstances in which hard practical help is demanded, and it is on their ability to provide this that the rest of what they have to offer will be judged. If the educational technologist cannot provide (personally or from some point within his organisation) a service which will lead to the desired outcome, then he can virtually forget any thoughts about educational or staff development.

'Educational development' and 'staff development' are buzz words current in the latter part of the 1970s. I use them because they have currency, but whatever terms are used they express a belief fundamental to most thinking and writing in the field of educational technology — that as the world changes around us the demands on education change, and educational technology has something to offer in its moves towards developing more appropriate modes of teaching and learning. This is not to say that we should sweep change across the face of education like some ideological Ghengis Khan. We should support the appropriate and replace the inappropriate. In each case the improvement and development of education will require service support.

It can therefore be argued that one way to ensure that educational technology secures an influence on the teaching and learning processes is to devise strategies whereby the most visible products, the media, will reduce suspicion and encourage involvement in the development of new materials as part of curriculum or methodological development. There are many examples of oblique approaches. In a college of education students were induced into thinking about the utilisation of low-technology resources without ever being told the objectives of the exercise. A large-scale, vertical, magnetic chessboard (a metal-backed board with the pieces made out of card and backed by adhesive magnetised rubber) was left in the students' common room. A plastigraph board and pieces demonstrating the principles of mathematical sets were set up in the concourse and students were left to play with this. A blackboard was set up in a corridor and a staff member who was expert at good chalk writing left a few lines on it. Within a short space of time the following results emerged; the students demanded more chessboards but also began to use the magnet board techniques in their teaching practice (a transference had been made), and students who had been incapable of grasping the principle of sets were prepared to learn through the game, transferring both the knowledge and the method into the schools. The blackboard soon became covered in graffiti, but beautifully written, and success was judged to be complete when all the verses of a poem about a certain Eskimo lady appeared in carefully executed copperplate.

Whilst such subterfuges should be continued, and staff can surely devise many others, a more systematic approach can be taken. As part of the National Development Programme for Computer Assisted Learning, the director Richard Hooper drew up a set of strategies for assimilation and dissemination of innovation. We can draw up a similar scheme, freely adapted from his work, which might provide a useful model for use within an institution.

Fundamental to any set of strategies is the notion that any new ideas, any innovation, any attempt to change people's attitudes, takes time. This time-lag between the presentation of an idea and its acceptance can be respresented by an 'S' curve, as is shown below.

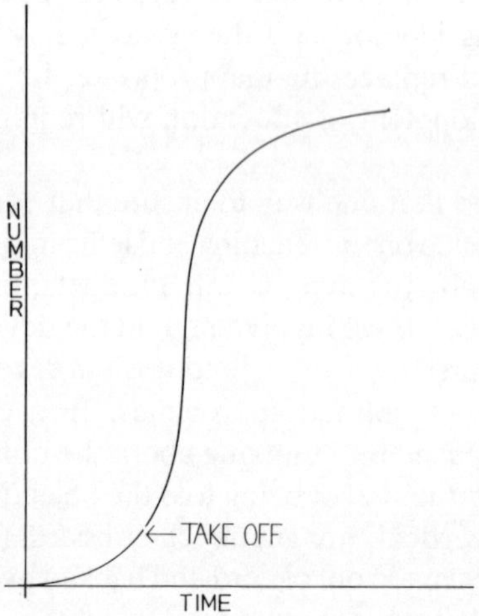

The flattened toe of the curve represents that period during which an idea is being propagated. It is generally recognised that once about 10% of the potential audience/users have accepted the idea the notion will gain critical mass and its large-scale acceptance will rise rapidly. In industrial and commercial terms periods of twenty years or more are common between the innovation and its acceptance. Many variables come into play. Television may have achieved critical mass in this country with the last coronation — many years after broadcasting began. Educational ideas are notorious for taking a long time to assimilate, and it is only after ideas have been assimilated that the notions begin to spread further through dissemination. Programmed learning reached a peak (in terms of the number of articles published) in about five years from the late 1950s, but it was another ten years before one could say that its principles became absorbed and assimilated into education. It was as long ago as the 1630s that Comenius wrote, 'Let it be given into the hands of children to delight themselves with the sight of pictures' — an attitude which has taken a long time to achieve critical mass.

How then can one set about persuading staff of the educational value of the outcomes of the educational technology services? How can one create changes of attitudes, re-examinations of present methodologies, without appearing to pose a threat to the autonomy and professional status of colleagues? The UNESCO model is based on the statement 'First find your enthusiast', the basis of which is to take the person who is already an enthusiast for resource-based learning and provide a large measure of support for their work. The hope is that by raising the profile of their alternative approach others will become interested in applying the same principles. This is sometimes described as the epidemic model, treating educational technology and its resulting new educational techniques as something infectious. Such a notion has many supporters in those who see education as a culture dish into which one implants a spore, for under laboratory conditions the spore will spread out over the surface of the dish and eventually cover it completely. However there are those who, when examining the circumstances in which they have to operate, do not see the institution as a uniform medium in a culture dish. The education body is made up of human beings, who, because of their differing natures, strengths and weaknesses, act as antibodies, and it has been found by some who have tried to implement innovation that support for the enthusiast is counter-productive. The infective model does not always work. The enthusiast is already seen as a person apart by the non-enthusiast, and any support given to the already active can serve to increase the differences between people, forcing the less adventurous further back into their tried and traditional mode of operation. The alternative approach is to seek out the least innovative, the most traditional, and try to alter their attitudes through practical support. This is a much more difficult approach but one which the practitioners who have had some success in this field are convinced produces longer-lasting results.

This experience was achieved to some extent by two critical points that have been made against high-cost schemes which have been injected into the system at apparently fertile growth points. Many projects in schools backed by national schemes in both the UK and the USA have had as their aim 'the development of high quality teaching materials based on appropriate definition of educational objectives and sound curriculum design...' Many of these school projects have assumed, and on occasion claimed, that the existence of high-quality teaching materials, positive research data, or elegant theoretical explications will ensure the assimilation of the particular innovation. This is rarely so, and in some cases these very factors have militated against the acceptance of an idea. (Richard Hooper, in an address to the 1977 ETIC Conference).

Similarly the Carnegie Commission on Higher Education in 1972 stated: 'One of the great disappointments of the national effort to date is that for all the funds and effort this expended for the advancement of instructional technology, penetration of the new learning materials and media into higher education has this far been shallow.' Perhaps the most illuminating comment of all can be found in the UNCAL Report of 1975, for although the main concern of the report is with computer-assisted learning the remarks could well apply to all aspects of educational technology: '... The citadel of established practice will seldom fall to the polite knock of a good idea; it may, however, yield to a long siege, a pre-emptive strike, a wooden horse or a cunning alliance.' It is to the wooden horse and the cunning alliance that we shall look in our consideration of Richard Hooper's strategies of assimilation and dissemination. Assimilation will for our purposes be defined as the process whereby we get innovations accepted by the individual or department, dissemination being the process whereby these notions are spread to others to that they might assimilate them.

Assimilation

Choice of Location of Activity

Try to locate any innovative project away from the educational technology unit, within a particular department and as close as possible to the departmental decision-makers. In this way the department may be actively involved and have a sense of commitment to the project, the outcome of which is for their own consumption.

Organisational Structure

Take great care over the co-operative structure that is established with a department for any project. It can be central to assimilation that there is as little as possible to gum up the works and that the power resides with those best able to influence others and carry through the decisions.

Co-operative Funding

The degree to which anyone within an institution is charged for any work varies greatly depending on the type of body and the financial structure, but where possible try to ensure that the individual or department has a financial stake in the activity. It will motivate them to become involved in the initial decision-making process and through to the final evaluation.

Critical Mass

The strategy of critical mass is essential for national and inter-institutional projects. It is more difficult to operate with the smaller numbers within an institution. However, apart from being the number required for 'take-off' it is premised on the belief that the more widespread the innovation the more it will acquire a broad base of support and visibility and the harder it will be to stop. One word of caution must be injected with regard to the strategy of critical mass; if an idea is 'bad' and achieves take-off it is just as likely to gain widespread acceptance as an idea that is 'good'.

Curriculum Integration

The strategy of curriculum integration tries to ensure that developments happen within the framework of broader curriculum and resource design. This is to avoid the innovation being regarded as an optional extra. It may be wise to place a high priority for the commitment of the support services, to any member of staff or department, on those projects which are either central to the existing curriculum or are part of curriculum renovation exercises. (Flemming and Coles of Southampton University have successfully used curriculum innovation as a strategy for staff development — see Coles, 1977.)

Riding the Educational Wave

This refers to the need to develop innovations that reinforce existing trends within the educational system. Thus within an institution the support is likely to be most effective when it is either developing trends that have already been recognised within that body or is bringing into play innovations that are currently recognised within the larger field of education. But of course, as in surfing, choosing the right wave is important; some waves look all right but are, in Australian surfing parlance, 'dumpers'.

Closing the Programme

One of the strongest strategies for assimilation is the planned closure of the project or programme. It should be clear to both parties in any co-operative venture involving the educational technology support that financial and time limits have been set — this tends to concentrate the minds on both sides of the project.

From the foregoing we can see that though we have up to this point been considering the educational technology services as *services*, the process of interaction with others is concerned with the spread of ideas, the possibility of assisting the improvement of the educational process. If one considers dissemination as a systematic attempt to promote the spread and adoption of new ideas and practices, it is clearly a part of the process of change. Hooper states that 'dissemination is amongst other things, a useful mechanism for testing the resilience and worth whileness of an innovation.' When considering the dissemination of ideas within an institution two distinct aspects can be seen, the first being a sort of publicity exercise, the spread of recognition of the educational and professional value of the support services, and the second being the spread of principles. While any one idea, based on our notion of activity being founded on practical support for particular needs, may result in the creation of learning resources or patterns of activity related to one department and even to a very specific part of the curriculum, our main concern should be for the spread of the ideas or principles embodied therein. A package may not be transferable across subject or departmental boundaries but the ideas should be. Any innovation which is so subject-specific that there is nothing for anyone else to learn from it has probably missed something in its development.

Dissemination

Inter-Departmental Projects

Where possible the involvement of staff from more than one department should be encouraged. This encourages the idea of dissemination being seen as part of development rather than an afterthought. Some projects will lend themselves readily to the involvement of other educationalists, evaluators, psychologists, etc. Inter-disciplinary projects may be more difficult to generate. One should not hesitate to look outwards to inter-institutional projects, as inter-institutional involvement of subject departments will assist in the broader process of dissemination and will raise the political profile of the project. The acceptability of a project will be increased if the people to whom it is directed have been involved in its development. It could reduce the power of the 'not-invented-here' syndrome and it allows for the differing values and opinions of the participants to be voiced early on the process.

Personal Contact

Here Hooper quotes House, who wrote in 'The Politics of Educational Innovation' in 1974 that 'To control the flow of personal contact is to control innovation. As the flow of blood is essential to human life so direct personal contact is essential to the propagation of innovation ... Who knows whom and who talks to whom are powerful indicators of where and when an innovation is accepted, or if it is accepted at all.'

Involvement with human personalities and institutional politics can neither be avoided nor ignored. The degree to which the support services receive the authoritative support of those in power will be amplified along the chains of responsibility within the establishment. The resource organiser responsible to a departmental head within a college, rather than to the Principal, will find it much harder to move, or gain acceptance (horizontally across subject boundaries, or vertically in the staff structure) in his or her need for personal contact. Support from the top is essential, not as a club with which to beat the backs of reluctant colleagues but as a key to open doors, avoiding some of the problems of status and lessening the degree to which conflicting pressures and direction can be applied.

Existing Communication Channels

Personal contact can be strengthened by exploitation of the existing communications channels used within the institution. In addition to any published or displayed communications channels are the more important and more powerful channels, the committees. Where possible educational technology, in whatever guise and under whatever name, should be present on those committees which govern the distribution of resources, take educational policy decisions, and control curriculum development. If subordinate to any departmental voice, educational technology will lose its power to take part in the most influential aspects of policy-making. This leads one to consider that the place for the support unit is completely outside any departmental structure, responsible to a point as high as possible within the directorial structure. The aim is not to give the educational technologist any unjustifiable status or power but to ensure that the support services are seen as having the approval of the institution's directorate and to allow for free movement between departments without any sense of threat or intrusion.

Presentation Skills

The presentation skills of the educational technologist (and those that are trained through the support service) are an often over-worked component of dissemination strategy. Presentation skill is not necessarily synonymous with the slickest of professional presentation; indeed there are some who think that in educational circles slick presentation can be counter-productive.

Portability

Whether we are considering technical or intellectual portability, it will be difficult to promote dissemination if what is developed cannot be easily transported from one educational situation to another.

The Exchange Agency

The creation of the awareness of the educational technology unit as an exchange unit can be a vital factor in the process of dissemination, by becoming the clearing-house for news and ideas about educational development. Through this function and in conjunction with the information base in the resource library the exchange can assist in a wide range of functions including standards setting, in-service training, consultancy, salesmanship and the encouragement of new software development.

Though these strategies have been freely adapted from Richard Hooper's original there is one quote with which he rounds off the exposition which is worthy of our application to the institutional context:

> There are inevitable tensions between assimilation and dissemination. We have to ensure that ideas are assimilable before we can attempt dissemination. It appears that assimilation is a necessary precondition for dissemination but that dissemination is not usually a necessary precondition for assimilation.

Staffing and Staff Organisation

It is the experience of many who operate in the field of educational technology that one is frequently required to make presentations to groups within education. However much one may suspect the value of evangelical pronouncements it is undeniable that they do have a part to play. The snares that lie in the undergrowth for the unwary trap those with a facility for evangelising into believing that this is all one has to do. One can preach an analytical approach to particular sets of circumstances or needs and advocate the systematic construction of a solution, yet one is still faced with the earnest enquirer who, over the brim of the teacup after the presentation, acknowledges the illumination that has been provided by one's edifying address and then asks the question 'But could you give me a list of what equipment/staff/software/space/money I will need to set up my resource centre?'

There are no valid prescriptive lists. So varied are the circumstances that prevail within any one institution that it is impossible to lay down any rules as to the staff that are required in order to provide a support service. Political and financial constraints may be seen as the major controlling factors for the development of a service, but there can be little hope for any successful implementation of an audio-visual or educational technology unit if there is not a wholehearted support and understanding from the most senior administrators. Not only is this support essential but the reasons for that support are crucial. There may, in the past, have been some loose talk about television units having been established because of the status that this gives to a college, and the fact that an equivalent institution has invested in a facility may become the rationale for a similar investment. One suspects that the working life of people who have then to run that facility can become an uphill struggle because of the lack of real comprehension of what the unit should be doing and the objectives that it should be striving to achieve.

I would argue that since the administration has control of investment and staffing it is that very administration which should be charged with setting the broad objectives of any support service. The administrators will then be in a position to judge the level of staffing and equipping required and will be accountable for the success or failure of the unit to meet the set objectives and the expectations of the rest of the staff. Knowing the objectives and the expected outcomes of the unit, the administrators can then determine the staff provision. Many colleges have to operate within complex rules of establishments. Decisions may have to be made as to the placing of educational technology staff on academic scales or on other non-academic gradings. As far as can be ascertained and judging by the divided opinions on this issue, this is one of those cases in which all the possible anwers are wrong. Staff given academic status feel freer to interact with, and receive recognition from, their academic colleagues but at the same time are caught by the jungle of formulae related to student numbers and departmental hierarchies. Those given non-academic status avoid these complications and may have greater security of tenure but find themselves under suspicion, lacking as they apparently do any academic status, the minute they seek to become involved with any pedagogical or curricular matters. It is a matter of great concern to many in educational technology posts that this dilemma has rarely been resolved. Administrators could well give serious consideration to the long-term effects of the status they give to the educational technology staff, as their perception of this role and status may not be shared by the rest of the academic staff and this can affect the progress of development and change.

As an alternative to a prescribed list of the staff required we can examine the roles that might be expected from a support service. The following list covers *some* but not necessarily all the roles that might be required:

Management
Educational Technologist
Resource Organiser
Financial Controller
Secretary/Typist
Schedule Planner

Equipment Control
Electronic Technician
Mechanical Technician
General Technician
Projectionist

Software Control
Librarian
Assistant Librarian
Library Assistant
Clerical Support
Delivery/Retrieval Staff

Professional Support
Adviser
Evaluator
Writer

Graphics
Graphic Artist
Technical Artist
Typography Designer
Layout Designer

Photographics
Photographer
Printer
Slide Mounter
Plate Printer

Printing
Typesetter
Layout Designer
Printer
Collater/Binder

		Technician
		Assistant
		Stores Manager
Audio	*Video*	*Film*
Recordist	Producer	Producer
Mixer	Clerical Worker	Cameraman
Editor	Electronics Engineer	Sound Recordist
Copier	Cameraman	Electrician
	Sound Operator	Camera Assistant
	Vision Mixer	Editor
	Camera Controller	Technician
	Recordist	Grip
	Lighting Designer	P.A.
	Designer	

Some of these roles might well be known by other names and there will be readers who could readily add further roles to the list. No quantities are placed against these titles, for the number will become a function of the size of the unit. The Open University may have thirty people in its graphics unit and still have to put a proportion of the work out to freelance artists. A college might have its graphics work done by the resource organiser in his lunch and tea breaks. The function of such a list is to indicate the types of role that will be required of the staff within a support service. Therefore if a decision is to be made to enter into any of these areas cognisance should be given to the implications for staffing. Let us take it as axiomatic that no matter how many staff are provided the work will expand beyond their capacity. Any resource organiser will say that his unit is under-staffed if he thinks there is a chance of getting any more manpower. Most will argue that more staff are needed simply to cope with the work in hand, knowing full well that additional staff never simply cope with the excess work but also create new capabilities which in turn become stretched beyond the point of efficiency.

The art of staff management is to create that level of staffing which can just deal efficiently with the demand but at the same time is sufficiently extended to be fully employed and prevent *ad hoc* random growth of a unit's operations. In an ideal world expansion should be carefully planned, costed, staffed and evaluated, and our less than ideal situation is amply demonstrated once we turn our attention to the smaller units in tertiary education. Large institutions usually receive high capital input and reasonably high levels of staffing, but the smaller colleges (and even departments which for one reason or another require their own support units) suffer badly. There are many colleges in which the majority of the functions listed earlier are expected from one man and a technician. Clearly there are many of these roles that will not merit the full-time employment of one person. A photographer may carry out all the functions listed under photography, and a printer may do all the jobs listed under printing. What is sometimes chastening is to see the vast amount of work that *can* be achieved by skilled and highly motivated individuals. I have visited a number of colleges and witnessed admirable organisation and enviable production all done by one person with the occasional support of a technician and a friendly soul in the secretarial office. The danger is that such success is held up as an example of what can be achieved through dedication and is then taken by onlookers as the staffing norm. For the poor lecturer who has the role of resource organiser thrust upon him, life can be very difficult. Few can achieve by themselves the sort of success that has been cited, and the failure to produce results can result in serious damage to the individual's health and career and the credibility of educational technology.

Administrators surely have a moral responsibility to treat educational technology with respect. If you do not believe in the implications of educational technology as a change agent then you should not attempt to introduce it into the institution, even in its crudest form of audio-visual aids. If you do have faith in the branching opportunities for change created by the introduction of media and a host of alternative methodologies, then the moral responsibility translates itself into a duty to ensure that adequate staffing is provided for those services which are chosen as appropriate and at a level which will allow attainment of the expected goals.

The status of the staff will affect their ability to carry out the tasks assigned, but spurious status is damaging to the whole system if it sets up expectations which can never be satisfied. It is somewhat depressing to receive communications from someone with a grand title such as Senior Lecturer in Educational Technology only to discover that he is alone in attempting to respond to all the demands of a college and that not only does he not have the time to lecture on Educational Technology but that there is no call for him to do so. The status of individuals can be matched by the status given to educational technology as a whole. As was stated earlier the subordinate role of a unit within a department robs it of the ability to cross subject boundaries, so that it can no longer be seen as the physical manifestation of an approach to education which is relevant to all subjects. If the administrators can create for the educational technology unit a separate identity then the process of dissemination of ideas can be eased. There are those who would argue that it is also essential to give the head of such a unit very senior status but this may not always be necessary. If the staff are given the mark of being specialists by the way they are treated by the administration then there need not necessarily be any barriers to approaching a head of a department who carries a higher status than oneself.

One strategy for creating the best attitude towards the educational technologist and all he stands for also happens to be one of the elements which is essential if the educational technologist is to move from a purely responsive, supportive role into that of the educational developer. This is *involvement.* By involving the educational technologist in those policy-making committees and groups that have an effect on teaching and learning, what is being offered will be more likely to be perceived by others as something essential to the whole development of education. It is surely better to involve the educational technologist at the begining of a curriculum development exercise rather than go through the whole process and then bring him in at the end as a sort of afterthought. One cannot be surprised if this latter model produces conflict.

If the educational technologist and the support services have the backing of those in authority and this is recognised by the rest of the staff then the conditions are right for the next step — educational development.

7 EDUCATIONAL DEVELOPMENT

Once services have been offered and received, once the facilities have been provided for others to produce their own resources, and once there is involvement in the process of learning, then there will be a need for in-service training. The introduction of media into the educational context will inevitably create a demand for courses on how to handle hardware. This alone, a simple course on equipment handling, may be the key to open the doors of suspicion and resistance. Just as education in recent years has had to acknowledge the existence of the calculator and the computer, so there should no longer be any Luddite resistance to the paraphernalia of audio-visual aids. Projectors and recorders exist and where appropriate can be used to improve learning. Of course one can teach without recourse to any tools other than one's own voice, but if educators are to think of themselves as professionals then it is not unreasonable to expect them to want to improve their professional skills.

The demand for in-service training in the handling of equipment provides the strategy for the introduction of many aspects of educational technology. To begin with it might be wise to hide the real objectives of such courses if one takes professional development as one of them. If for the sake of argument we can take a rather loose definition of educational development we can then see how the strategy of in-service training can be one of the methods of achieving such ends.

Educational development encompasses:

(a) Staff development — improving the professional knowledge and skills of staff (see Coles, 1977).
(b) Curriculum development — improving the understanding of the processes and systems involved.
(c) Evaluative development — improving the systems of judgement which in turn affect (a) and (b).

Within each of these areas there are elements that appear to fall within the province of various professional groups, e.g. the 'media people', the psychologists, etc. If we were to enter the lists with challenges as to who should carry out educational development we would be back once more in the divisive ground that we examined at the beginning of this book. What matters is that educational development is carried out by *somebody*, and as has been noted several times there need be few cases in education of mutual exclusivity. I believe that there are many areas of staff development for which an educational technology unit or a media support unit would be ideally suited, but I also believe with equal strength that there are very few things that such units can do alone. Educational technology can shoulder much of the burden but must share the overall task with the equally essential skills of the subject specialist, the educational psychologist, the evaluator, the methods specialist and so on.

My belief that one should take an oblique or covert approach to educational development is premised on the evidence of the experience of most of the people interviewed during the preparation of this book, and on the same view expressed in the writing of many others. Whereas in many walks of life high priority is given to the improvement of professional expertise there appears to be a sense of resistance to this concept in education. Terms such as 'educational development' or 'staff development' are seen as threats by many who feel that they have gained their positions through professional excellence, and the establishment of an educational development unit is clearly viewed by some as implying a deficit in their ability. Whilst we may view such an attitude as arrogance we cannot deny that people feel this way. If they feel it they will act as though the threat was real and reject what is being offered. One cannot approach colleagues head-on, like a bull in a china-shop, and say 'I am now going to develop your professional skills', for that is as arrogant as their assumption that their skills cannot be developed. One has to recognise that exercises of this type do pose a genuine threat in that if they are not handled properly the weaknesses of colleagues may be exposed to public scrutiny. One has also to recognise that no one 'improves' other people; the process of development occurs in the individual as a result of the context and content of the exercise provided by others. One therefore has to set out to create a set of conditions in which, in one sense, colleagues can improve themselves and educational development can take place.

Coles argues that courses are inappropriate for professional development, which he sees as taking place over specific issues within the particular staff member's own context through the close involvement of the educational technologist. Whilst one sees the virtue of this in the later stages of the process there has to be a strategy for initiating the process in the first place and securing the co-operation of members of staff. It would seem reasonable to begin with some centrally organised courses. The least threatening of these, and one which might well be viewed by the sceptic as being the province of the support unit, is the course on equipment handling. If a range of simple courses is offered there may be very few takers, therefore a dual approach has been successfully adopted by some colleges. The first is the induction course. With the support of the administration you can set up a series of basic courses which must be taken by all new members of staff (preferably by *all* staff no matter what their previous experience). In this way you will at least be sure that some staff know how to use equipment correctly and safely. The second part of the strategy is to conduct similar courses within departments but with the course content tailored to the specific demands of the staff. This will require close liaison with departmental heads but will have the added advantage of tackling real issues that are relevant to the staff concerned, rather than the less effective concentration on generalities.

In both cases there are some guidelines to be followed.

(a) Make the courses simple. Don't present the processes in such a way that the equipment is seen to be complicated. As educational technologists we should be sufficiently secure to de-mystify the things we deal with, but far too often we build up a mystique around our working tools and scare off the learner. After all most audio-visual equipment is sold on the domestic market and is easily operated by children, so why do adults have difficulties? Sewing machines and cars are far more complicated than any audio-visual equipment yet many staff use sewing machines, and haven't you noticed how many complete idiots can drive cars?

(b) Make the courses as relevant as possible. Choose equipment and examples as close to the staff involved as possible and then make the courses *practical*. Ten minutes of practical workshop experience are better than hours of theoretical explanation. (How often does one come across people *talking* about the use of audio-visual resources for learning?)

(c) Maintain the right to fail. During courses it is essential that staff are made aware that they will not lose face by making mistakes. The right to fail is sacrificed as soon as they transfer the techniques back to the teaching context, but if they have the bolt-hole of the right to fail during the course then their sense of personal security is less threatened and the chances of them giving some commitment to the work are increased.

Once staff have become involved in learning about the hardware then two things follow. It is difficult to envisage any course on hardware that does not involve considerations of software and a course is surely deficient if the uses of both hardware and software are not related to the reasons why one chooses to use particular media and the effects this might have. Thus whilst one may be offering what is ostensibly a hardware course it can be the mechanism whereby staff become involved in questions of software selection, software production,and development of appropriate methodology and evaluation. Whilst this process begins with the hardware it is a method of assisting staff towards a recognition of the process:

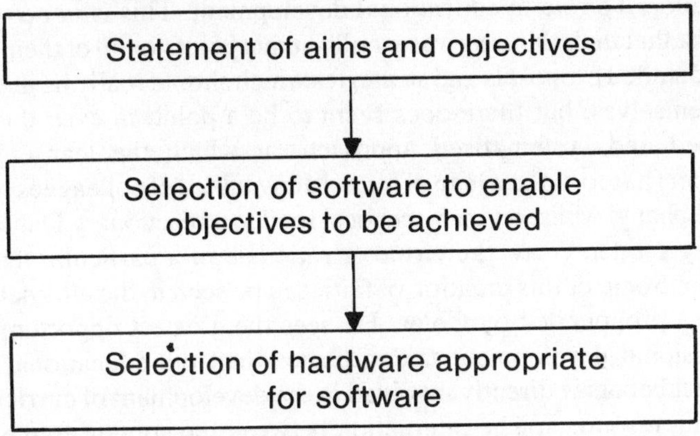

In practice this process is more complex and, depending on the course content and complexity, may have many feedback loops for the evaluation of learning from the selected media, evaluation of the course and the method, and reassessment of the objectives. The step from the simple course to the more complex developmental exercise can become an organic growth if the appropriate relationships are established in these early stages.

Once this step has been taken and staff have awarded some credibility to the educational technology unit, courses can be introduced on the various methodologies and techniques of teaching. One uses the word 'courses' with some hesitation because one is now moving into that difficult area in which one is deliberately making affective changes in colleagues. If courses are to be conducted on presentation techniques, lecturing skills, the conduct of seminars, the structuring and writing of individualised learning, then the educational technologist should not necessarily assume that he is the best person to do all or any of these jobs. Within an institution it should not be difficult to discover which individuals are the most skilled in presenting and transferring skills — the best lecturer is not necessarily the best person to teach lecturing skills. Where possible, involve these people in the programme of educational development and try to make them insiders within your team. It will help increase the faith of those you are aiming to convert.

The above words are chosen deliberately, for it was noticeable when conducting interviews with a wide range of educational technologists as background to this book that almost all of them began to use theological terminology once we began to discuss the educational technologist's role in educational development. This is in no way to suggest that their thinking was woolly at this point, for all of them could offer detailed proposals and strategies which should really be in a book by themselves, but there does seem to be a point, in even the most detailed and systematised approach, at which the learner (staff member) has to make a leap of faith. Many talked of colleagues having an 'epiphany' whilst on their sceptical road to a reactionary Damascus, as they suddenly saw the virtue or rationale of a particular learning system. Some of this creation of faith can be seen in the alternative to courses propounded by Coles. He sees the greatest opportunity for professional development taking place when the educational technologist becomes directly involved in the development of curricula or learning resources. The interaction between the content-free educational technologist and the content specialist is the point at which development takes place. He sees this as the process of the 'outsider' becoming the 'insider'. This is not unlike the adoption of faith since it implies belief in the value of the 'outsider'. I would only add that *one* way the 'outsider' can create the credibility which engenders the leap of faith which in turn lowers the drawbridge of suspicion is to be the most efficient and effective provider of appropriate services. Credible support which is not seen as a threat can become the firm foundation on which new and as yet unknown development can be built.

8 SUMMARY

This book has presented an outline of the way that educational technology support services can be developed and managed within an institution of tertiary education. Many aspects of educational technology have received either no mention at all or at best short shrift. It was not the purpose of this work to consider such crucial issues as evaluation and the many alternative methodologies, as other books have been and will be written on these aspects.

No consideration has been given to the place of computers or the micro-chip with all its promises of educational, industrial and social change. Nevertheless it is my contention that, no matter what the changes are that follow on from this post-industrial revolution and no matter what evolves from the present intellectual and academic concerns, there will always be resources of some kind that have to be efficiently organised if education is to benefit from their existence. There will always be the need for support services to those who teach and learn.

If we are to take the notion from the computer-assisted learning specialists that 'instrumentation alters orientation' and re-express it as 'media alter methods' then the educational technologist will have an increasingly important role in education in a world which is continuing to create media as information carriers at an ever-increasing rate. No matter which of the roles or definitions cited in the appendix of this book one chooses as one's framework for being an educational technologist, there will be a role for the support service organiser. It is the contention of this book that one of the most effective strategies for infiltrating the core of education is through the service entrance. It is my belief that effective support can create effective change.

To make that support effective one has to establish the best possible systems within the given context, realising that every decision has long-term implications. One should attempt to make those choices that will, in the long term, result in the educationalist becoming the 'insider' rather than the 'outsider'.

In the words of the prologue:

> 'It pays to look where you are going.'

BIBLIOGRAPHY

Organisation and management of resources is so dependent on variables that there is no list of books that can be considered as holding the authoritative view. There are a great many valuable and valued opinions and each reader will have to pick out those aspects which seem to be most appropriate for their particular circumstances and predictions. Reading through the books listed is a form of game, a search for a critical path. Many of the quoted works themselves contain extensive bibliographies which can set up new avenues of investigation.

Ader, Jean, *Building Implications of the Multi-option School,* programme on educational buildings (OECD, 1975). The problems faced by the developers of the multi-option school provide much useful guidance for Further Education and Higher Education.

AECT, *Basic Guidelines for Media and Technology in Teacher Education* (Association for Educational Communications and Technology, 1975). Though based on American experience, a useful reference work for those concerned with teacher training.

——, *Media Centres: Readings from Audio-Visual Instruction* (Association for Educational Communications and Technology, 1975). A collection of typically terse articles from 'Audio-Visual Instruction'.

Audio Visual Facilities for New School Buildings, an administrator's checklist (The New Hampshire Audio Visual Association, 1, 1963). A checklist for both new and upgraded schools.

Barnes, Neil H., *BBC Further Education: A report on the use of broadcasts in further education colleges* (BBC, 1976). This raises questions about the under-use of broadcasts as an educational resource.

Baume, A.D. and Jones, B., *Education by Objectives: How to use aims and objectives in course design, development and operation,* curricular study 1 (Nelpress, 1974).

Beard, Ruth, *Teaching and Learning in Higher Education*, Penguin Education Special (Penguin Books, 1970). Though much has changed since 1970, there are clear pointers on the implications of alternative methodologies.

Beswick, Norman, *School Resource Centres — Schools Council Working Paper 43*(Evans/Methuen Educational, 1972).
——*Organising Resources* (Schools Council Publications, 1975). These two books together provide a central work on the organisation of resources in schools. Although emphasising the library aspects and occasionally indulging in fence-sitting, these books are brimfull of facts and ideas applicable to any situation in which learning resources have to be organised. There are particularly good bibliographies in these volumes.
Beynon, John, *Study Carrels, designs for independent study space,* (EFL, New York, 1968). Contains 16 examples of designs for carrels.
Bomar, Cora P. *et al.* (eds.), *Guide to the Development of Educational Media Selection Centres* (American Library Association, Chicago Il 60611, 1973).
Briault, E., *Allocation and Management of Resources in Schools* (Council for Educational Technology, London, 1974). The principles of management are as appropriate to tertiary education as they are to the schools considered in this work.
Brown, Joan D., *The Development of Educational Technology in Colleges of Education* (Councils and Education Press, London, 1970). A contribution to the issue of the development of educational technology in teacher training, a central issue if genuine assimilation is to take place.
Brown, J.W. and Thornton, J.W. (eds.), *New Media in Higher Education* (NEA, Washington, 1963). Once again, though American in origin there are papers of interest and value to those working in other systems.
Bruner, Jerome S., *Toward a Theory of Instruction* (Harvard University Press, 1966).
Brynmor Jones (Chairman) 1965, *Audio Visual Aids in Higher Scientific Education* (The Brynmor Jones Report) H.M.S.O. London.
Building Bulletins (H.M.S.O., 1968). An extensive series of special bulletins has been produced by The Department of Education and Science.
Carlson, Richard O., *Adoption of Educational Innovation* (Center for the Advanced Study of Educational Administration, University of Oregon, 1965).
Carnegie Foundation, *The Fourth Revolution: Instructional Technology in Higher Education* (McGraw-Hill, 1972).
Clarke, John, *Learning Resources for an Institution of Higher*

Education: A Feasibility Study (Dundee College of Education, 1978). A detailed survey by the Co-ordinator of Learning Resources of the development, production and utilisation of resources in a college of education.

Coles, C.R., 'Developing Professionalism: Staff Development as an Outcome of Curriculum Development', *PLET*, vol. 14, no. 4, (November 1977).

Collier, K.G., Hodge, H.P.R., Horton, T.F., Rathborn, M., *Working Paper No. 5, Colleges of Education Learning Programmes: A Proposal* (NCET, 1971).

Community/School: Sharing the Space and the Action (Educational Facilities Laboratories, 1973, second printing 1974). A consideration of alternative use of spaces and the methods that are implicit in the change. This approach leads towards the school without walls and thence to distance learning.

Coppen H., *A Survey of British Research in Audio-Visual Aids 1945-1967* (plus annual supplements) (National Committee for Audio-Visual Aids in Education, London, 1968). Essential reference work.

Dale, Edgar, *Audiovisual Methods in Teaching* (Holt, Rinehart and Winston, 1946-69). The American standard introductory text for many. Though it now looks a bit dated and is school-based there are few works with this amount of coverage of audio-visual media.

Davis, John A., 'What's Happened to Instructional Development in Our Universities?', in *Audio Visual Instruction* (February 1978).

Davies, I.K. and Hartley, J. (eds.),*Contributions to an Educational Technology* (Butterworth, London, 1972).

Davies, W.J.K., *Learning Resources? An Argument for School*, CET Guideline No. 1 (Council for Educational Technology, London, 1975). Though prepared for the primary and secondary school the detailed descriptions of low-cost solutions to practical and organisational problems provide a wealth of information.

Duncan, C.J. (ed.), *Modern Lecture Theatres* (Oriel Press, 1966). Guide to lecture theatre design in the UK.

Educational Technology: Progress and Promise (NCET). The report of the National Council for Educational Technology for the years 1967-73.

Educational Technology: The Design and Implementation of Learning Systems (OECD, 1971). Valuable papers based on a European Seminar on 'Educational Technology — Strategies for Implementation'. Of particular interest are the sections on production, staff training and agencies for innovation.

Eraut, Dr. Michael, Occasional paper No. 4, *In-service Education for Innovation* (NCET, 1972). The successful assimilation of innovations rarely happens by accident, training is required for the necessary skills.

Eraut, M. and Squires, G., *An Annotated Select Bibliography of Educational Technology,* 2nd edition (Council for Educational Technology, London, 1973). An essential reference work.

Erickson, C.W.H., *Fundamentals of Teaching with Audio-Visual Technology* (Collier-Macmillan, New York, 1972). An essential text for anyone with a concern for the implications for education once audio-visual aids are introduced.

Fairfax, Olivia, *British Library/Council for Educational Technology joint feasibility study into the development of a national cataloguing and information service for audio-visual materials* (May 1975). Anyone concerned with the efficient control of information should be aware of what is being proposed on a national basis.

—— (ed.), *Directory of Information Sources and Advisory Services in Educational Technology (CET, 1974).*

Fielden, J. and Pearson, P.K., The Cost of Learning with Computers, the report of the financial evaluation of the national development programme in computer assisted learning (CET, 1978).

Flood-Page, C.J., *Technical Aids to Teaching in Higher Education*, SRHE Monograph 15 (Society for Research in Higher Education, London, 1971).

Fothergill, R., *Resource Centres in Colleges of Education: National Council for Educational Technology Working Paper 10* (Council for Educational Technology, London, 1973). Richard Fothergill's study complements and adds to the other studies of resource centres in schools.

Gagne, R.M., *The Conditions of Learning*, 2nd edition (Holt, Rinehart and Winston, New York, 1970). This together with Gagne's other writings provides one of the most influential approaches towards the development of learning.

Gagne, R.M. and Briggs, Leslie J., *Principles of Instructional Design* (Holt, Rinehart and Winston, 1974).

Gardner, A., *Educational Technology: Midas Machine or Bottomless Pit* (Paper presented at ETIC, 1978).

Gardner, Dennis, *Developments in Communications: their implications for education* (CET, 1974). Seminar and conference reports.

A seminar held at Harrogate in June 1973.

Gnagey, W.J., Chesebro, P.A. and Johnson, J.A., *Learning Environments* (Holt, Rinehart and Winston, New York, 1972).

Gosling, W., *Microcircuits, Society and Education*, Occasional Paper 8, (CET, 1978). Professor Gosling explores some of the possible developments and social effects of microtechnology. Essential reading unless you believe that the micro-chip is just a passing fancy.

Green, Alan C. *et al.*, *Educational Facilities with New Media*, Report A: A guide for policy makers — Report B: A guide for the design professions — Report C: A technical guide (Rensselaer Polytechnic, New York, 1968).

Gross, N., Giacquinta, J.B. and Bernstein, M., *Implementing Organizational Innovations* (Harper and Row, New York, 1971). A most valuable work for the resource organiser or administrator, concerned as it is with organisation rather than the educational content.

Hall, William C., 'Pretending Not to Be an Educational Technologist'. *Programmed Learning and Educational Technology*, vol. 12, no. 6, (November 1975). An example of the healthy scepticism that occasionally appears in this important journal.

Hamilton, Jenkins, King, MacDonald and Parlett, *Beyond the Numbers Game: A Reader in Educational Evaluation* (Macmillan Education Ltd, 1977). As well as being a stimulating jumping-off point for a reader in evaluation, there is an extensive bibliography.

Harris, N.D.C., *Educational Technology in European Higher Education*, CET Seminar Report No. 2 (Council for Educational Technology, London, 1976).

Havelock, R.G., *The Change Agents Guide to Innovation in Education* (Educational Technology Publications, 1973).

—— *A Guide to Innovation in Education* (University of Michigan, 1970).

—— 'The Utilisation of Educational Research and Development', *British Journal of Educational Technology 2,* no. 2 (May 1971).

Havelock, Ronald G. and Havelock, Mary C., *Training for Change Agents: A guide to the design of training programs in education and other fields*, Center for Research on Utilization of Scientific Knowledge, Institute for Social Research (University of Michigan, 1973). Havelock, throughout most of his writing illuminates the role of the educational technologist through terms such as 'change agent' 'linker' or 'knowledge broker'. One feels that this essentially practical approach gets to the heart of the reality of the resource organiser's world.

Haviland, David S., 'Designing for Educational Technology', *AIA Journal*, (October 1970) (reprints). Has a very comprehensive bibliography.

—— *Multimedia Classrooms Revisited* (Rensselaer Polytechnic, New York, 1970).

Hicks, Warren B. and Tillin, Alma M., *Managing Multi-Media Libraries* (R.R. Bowker, New York, 1973).

Holder, M.L. and Mitson, R., *Resources Centres* (Methuen, 1974). Background material which is mainly concerned with principles. The authors initiated one of the most visited resource centres in Britain.

Holling, K.,'The Feedback Classroom', in Unwin, D. (ed.), *Media and Methods: Instructional Technology in Higher Education* (McGraw-Hill Book Company, Maidenhead, 1969).

Hooper, Richard, *The National Development Programme in Computer Assisted Learning*, final report of the Director (CET, 1977).

Hooper, Richard and Toye, Ingrid (eds.), *Computer Assisted Learning in the United Kingdom*, some case studies (CET, 1975). The National Development Programme has important ramifications into other non-computer developments of education. In particular the programme reveals much about the process of innovation.

Instructional Hardware: a guide to architectural requirements (EFL, 1970).

Knapper, C., *Evaluating Instructional Technology* (Croom Helm, London. To be published 1979).

Lamb, Brydon, *New Methods and Media in Further Education* (NCAVAE, 19).

Lewis B., in Malcolm, A.H. (ed.), 'A Resources Centre. . .is a state of mind' (Scottish Educational Film Association 1973).

Library Association Media Cataloguing Rules Committee, Working Paper No. 11, *Non-book materials: Cataloguing rules* (NCET and Library Association, 1973).

Macbeath, R.J., *Audio Visual Education: Methods and Materials* (Whitcombe and Tombs, Christchurch, 1967).

—— (ed.), *Extending Education Through Technology* (AECT, Washington, DC, 1972).

MacKenzie, M.L., *Deciding to Individualise Learning: A Study of the Process* (CET, 1978). This case study of the development of the study method at Dundee College of Education provides a detailed background to an example of innovation which should be of interest to all tertiary institutions.

Mackenzie, N. *et al.*, *Teaching and Learning — An Introduction to New Methods and Resources in Higher Education* (UNESCO and the International Association of Universities, Paris, 1970).

Mager, Robert F., *Preparing Instructional Objectives* (Fearon Publishers Inc., 1975). This and the other works by Mager may be considered essential reading as well as being fun to read.

Malcolm, A.H. *et al.*, 'A Resources Centre . . . is a state of mind' (Scottish Educational Film Association, 1973). Descriptions of school resources centres by the people who have established and run them.

Malcolm, A.H., *The Setting up of a Resources Centre: 1. Basic Ideas* (Scottish Educational Film Association, 1974).

Malcolm, A.H. (ed.), *The Setting up of a Resources Centre: 3. Retrieval Systems* (Scottish Educational Film Association, 1976). This series is based on practical experience in existing resource centres and is concerned to provide low cost organisation patterns. The ultimate aim is greater ease of access to resources and the more effective use of learning materials.

Meyer, Jan F., *Media Innovation and Faculty Change,* in *Audio Visual Instruction* (February 1978).

Microelectronics: Their Implications for Education and Training, A statement by the Council for Educational Technology (CET 1978).

NCAVAE/ACCT (joint working party, *Staffing and Training for Educational Closed-Circuit Television*, Working Paper No. 7 (NCET, 1971).

NCAVAE, *School Building Design and Audio-Visual Resources*, Central Council of Advisers in Audio-Visual Education and Central Committee of Teachers' Visual Aids Group (NCAVAE Visual Education Book Service, n.d.).

NCAVAE, *The Organisation of Audio-Visual Resources for Learning in a Local Education Authority* (NCAVAE Visual Education Book Service, London, n.d.).

NCAVAE, *The Training of Teachers and Educational Technology*, a report prepared on behalf of the Central Committee of Advisers in Audio-Visual Education and the Central Committee of Teachers' Visual Aids Groups (NCAVAE Visual Education Book Service, London, n.d.).

New Trends in the Utilization of Educational Technology for

Science Education (UNESCO Press, Paris 1974).

Nieme, J.A. (ed.), *Mass Media and Adult Education* (Educational Technology Publications, Englewood Cliffs, New Jersey, 1971).

Places and Things for Experimental Schools. A joint report from Educational Laboratories Inc. and Experimental Schools (February 1972).

Planning and Operating Media Centers. Readings from Audiovisual Instruction 2 (Association for Educational Communications and Technology, Washington, DC, 1975).

Postman, Neil and Weingartner, Charles, *Teaching as a Subversive Activity*, Penguin Educational Special (Penguin Books, 1969). If, as has been stated, instrumentation alters orientation we should question our assumptions — this book raises some of the necessary questions.

Propst, Robert, *High School: The Process and the Place*, Educational Facilities Laboratories (January 1972).

Reed, Elizabeth, *Support Staff for Educational Technology in Further and Higher Education*, 1977. An analysis (part of which is confidential) prepared for CET.

Richmond, W. Kenneth, *The Education Industry*, (Methuen, 1969).

Richmond, W. Kenneth (ed.), *The Concept of Educational Technology — a Dialogue with Yourself* (Weidenfeld and Nicolson, 1970). The various writings of Mr Richmond are nothing if not stimulating and would serve as an excellent starting point for a reader. One may not agree with all his ideas but cannot remain passive before them.

Rigg, Robinson P., *Audio Visual Aids and Techniques in Managerial and Supervisory Training* (Hamish Hamilton, 1969).

Rowantree, Derek, *Educational Technology in Curriculum Development* (Harper and Row, 1974). One of the major works on the place of educational technology in curriculum development, what might be called the heart of education itself. An extensive bibliography is included.

Shiffrin, M.R., *Information in the School Library: An Introduction to the Organisation of Non-Book Materials* (Bingley, London, 1973). A librarian's approach based on some of the best practical and theoretical work today. Just as valid for tertiary education.

Skinner, B.F., *The Technology of Teaching* (Prentice Hall, 1968). You do not always have to agree with Skinner. He represents those who attempt to take a thoroughly scientific approach. Skinner represents one segment of the spectrum which also includes the intuitive and non-scientific elements.

Smith, Peter, *The Design of Learning Spaces* (CET, 1974). The many examples cited here provide a wealth of good ideas together with a usefully grouped bibliography.

Suyder, B.R., *The Hidden Curriculum* (Knopf, 1971). A good introduction to the notion of the hidden curriculum. Any teacher should be aware of what might be being learned in spite of what is being taught.

Tansey, P.J. and Unwin, D., *Simulation and Gaming in Education* (Methuen, London, 1969). Gaming and simulation are important components of the larger structure of approaches to learning. This book provides a clear and informative introduction.

Taylor, George, *The Teacher as Manager* (NCET, 1970). Again, though concerned with school organisation, the papers from this symposium provide much valuable information for FE and HE institutions.

Taylor, L.C., *Resources for Learning*, Penguin Education Special (Penguin Books, 1971). Though most of this is concerned with schools there are many pointers for action in tertiary institutes, particularly the section on Independent Learning.

Thornton, James, and Brown, James (eds.), *New Media and College Teaching* (Association for Educational Communications and Technology, London, 1969).

Tucker, R.N., 'Excuse Me, Is This the Right Bandwagon?' in *Prcgrammed Learning and Educational Technology 3* (1975). Some thoughts on the development of resource centres and the findings of the UNESCO Working Party.

Tucker, R.N., *The Setting up of a Resources Centre: 2. Planning and Staffing* (Scottish Educational Film Association, 1976). Architectural and organisational case studies.

UNESCO, *Transformation of School Libraries into Multi-Media Centres (UNESCO, 1976).* The work cited in this book, although based quite strongly on the French approach to resource organisation provides a good structural model.

UNESCO, New Trends in the Utilization of Educational Technology for Science Education (UNESCO, 1974).

Unwin, D. (ed.), *Media and Methods — Instructional Technology in Higher Education* (McGraw-Hill, London, 1969). A major collection of papers which could open up many more avenues of research for a reader.

Verduin, J.R., *Conceptual Models in Teacher Education: An Approach to Teaching and Learning* (American Association of Colleges for Teacher Education, Washington, DC, 1967).

Walton, J. and Rusk, J. (eds.), *Resources and Resource Centres* (Ward Lock Educational, London, 1975). These editors, experienced themselves in organising resources, bring together an illuminating set of papers..

Weinstock, Ruth, *The Greening of the High School*. Conference co-sponsored by Educational Facilities Laboratories and Institute for Development of Educational Activities, Inc. (1973). A quirky production taking an idiosyncratic look at the American high school. Don't be put off by some of the language — there are exciting ideas hiding behind the words.

Wiman, R.V. and Meierhenry, W.C., *Educational Media: Theory into Practice* (Merrill, Columbus, Ohio, 1969).

Winslade, B.A.J. and Beswick, N.W., *Resource Centres: an Annotated Bibliography* (College of Librarianship, Wales 971). One of the best bibliographies on resources centres, arising as it does from one of the most experienced writers on the subject and the Library School which is, probably, most concerned with non-book media librarianship.

Wittich, W.A. and Schuller, C.F., *Instructional Technology: Its Nature and Use*, 5th ed. (Harper and Row, New York, 1973).

Wright, Andrew, *Training for Educational Media Design* Working Paper No. 9 (NCET, 1973).

GLOSSARY

'Above-the-line' Costing— the cost of the materials used in a job, together with any other actual costs. Costs of staff and institutional overheads are considered as 'below-the-line'.

'Best Buy' — a mythical concept, fostered by sectors of the consumer market, founded on the erroneous impression that all the customers are identical and that there is some substantial similarity between people's needs. There is no such thing, in education, as a universal best buy.

Bibliographic Control — the ordering, categorisation and classification of information utilising those skills, processes and modes of thought that have been developed by professional librarians. Though strictly applied to 'books' the term can now be used in the context of 'non-books' and information.

Compatibility — equipment which can handle one type of software is said to be compatible. A 16 mm film can be shown on any 16 mm projector. Such standardisation does not exist in the realm of video equipment and there is much concern over apparent problems of compatibility. Whilst there are sound arguments for standardisation, we should remember how materials can be transferred from one form to another, and worry less about mechanical compatibility and more about intellectual compatibility, i.e. having transferred the material do you actually want to listen to what it has to say?

Data Base — another borrowing from the world of the computer, and one which has lost its precision in the move. In the variable world of multi-media libraries and information storage the term 'database' has become an imprecise collective for the conglomeration of information.

Hardware (see also Software) — as with the term software, hardware has been borrowed from computer terminology. In audio-visual terminology it is now taken to mean the equipment, the machines, on which the materials (or software) are viewed or played.

Input — within a library or information system input is the combination of all the activities of data gathering, classifying and cataloguing, that go into the creation of the usable record in an appropriate form for the customer.

Institution — used here to cover the range of educational contexts. The concept of institution applies in the main to the organisational and administrative body rather than simply to the physical buildings.

Keywords — a set of terms by which information or catalogue items are ordered to enable the searcher to enter the record through a controlled vocabulary of words. The thesaurus of terms is often developed to meet specific subject needs or ability levels.

Language Laboratory — a description variously attributed to the room containing equipment and to the equipment itself, which is usually a series of booths equipped with tape recorders. The booths are connected to a master console. The mode of learning and interacting with the tape may vary. The use of the term 'language laboratory' has perhaps reduced the effectiveness of this particular arrangement of technology — it can be used for learning in many other subjects and should perhaps be termed a 'learning laboratory'.

Learning-by-appointment — a system of self-paced learning, using a modular course. This is a form of distance learning although conducted within the institution. The structure allows for shift-workers and those with work patterns that prohibit enrolment in regular timetabled courses to enter 'continuing education'.

Learning Materials — a collective term for books, audio-visual materials, work sheets, programmes, games, etc. which have been designed for the use of the learner. The carrier of the information is less important than the function for which it is designed.

Light Box — a surface illuminated from behind, on which transparencies, slides and filmstrips can be viewed. The simplest form might be strips of draught-excluder rubber stuck to a window. For large working surfaces plate glass and opalescent plastic over cold fluorescent lights are used.

Non-book — an example of using a term to describe its opposite. Unfortunately there is not yet a simple collective term to describe all those information carriers that are not in the traditional form of a book. The time must surely come soon when we cease to make a false distinction between one particular physical form and all the rest of the forms of media.

Non-commercial Sources — producers of resources not intended for large-scale production and sale. Usually these are institutions or resource production units. The term non-commercial does not necessarily imply a lower quality of production.

OHP — the overhead projector; more accurately called the retroprojector or over-the-shoulder projector in other languages. Designed to allow a large-scale display to be projected on to a screen whilst the teacher/presenter remains facing the audience. Surely one of the most abused items of visual equipment; on the simple principle that it makes things bigger and brighter the natural consequence is that it makes rubbish into bigger and brighter rubbish.

Output — within the context of the library or information system the output is taken as the usable record — the card catalogue or the specially created list.

Remote Control — usually used to refer to the placing of certain of the controls for equipment at a point some distance from the equipment. The controls usually found are, for the slide projector, forward/reverse and focus; and for radio and television, volume and channel selection. The majority are directly wired to the set. Newer developments of ultra-sonics and coded infra-red may allow for a wider range of control over more types of equipment including the room lighting.

Software (see also Hardware) — as with hardware, this term has been borrowed from computer terminology. In audio-visual terminology it is taken to mean the materials that are shown or played on the hardware.

Systematic — this term is taken to mean an organised approach or system. No attempt is made to prescribe that system, it is a process of thought or development based on a series of rational steps and deductive argument. It should not be confused with the use of the word 'systems' in the term 'a systems approach' which claims to have a much more closely defined set of rules, but as defined in the Encyclopedia of Educational Media Communications and Technology 'the terms systems approach is virtually meaningless'.

APPENDIX

The title of this book contains the words 'educational technology'. There are many definitions of educational technology.

'A systematic way of designing, carrying out and evaluating a total process of teaching and learning in terms of specific objectives based on findings from research in human learning and communications.'
(Report of US President's Commission of Enquiry)

'The process of applying the findings of behavioural psychology to the design of instruction.'
(Professor Glaser, Pittsburgh University)

'The development, application and evaluation of systems, techniques and aids in the field of human learning.'
(Report of DES Working Party on 'Central Arrangements for Promoting Educational Technology in the United Kingdom'.)

We think of educational technology as being a systematic approach to the effective implementation of the curriculum. We see educational technology as an attempt to formulate and apply a 'science of instruction'. Accordingly, we lay stress on the following factors —

- — the psychology of learning and teaching
- — theories of communication
- — course design and systems planning
- — practical skills associated with the production of resources material
- — management skills in education, particularly those associated with the management of innovation.

(D.C. Butts in a paper to the Scottish Council for Educational Technology)

1. Educational Technology is the adaptation of techniques of organisation, presentation and analysis to teaching and learning situations.

or

2. Educational Technology is the pragmatic use in the classroom of developments in curriculum innovation.

or

3. Educational Technology is the application of curriculum development in the classroom.

or

4. Educational Technology is the implementation of curriculum innovation.

(A.H. Malcolm in a paper to the Scottish Council for Educational Technology)

A systematic approach to designing and evaluating learning and teaching methods and methodologies and to the application and exploitation of media and of the current knowledge of communication techniques in education, both formal and informal.
(A working definition adopted by the Scottish Council for Educational Technology)

These are only a few of the many definitions that have been offered, each valuable and each made with a particular perspective of education. None of these is mutually exclusive of the others but to blend them together begins to produce a conception of educational technology that is so broad as to be in danger of being synonymous with education itself.

Consider the following three comments, the first and second expanding the definitions into more focused images of a spectrum of activities, the third being a salutary bucket of cold water from cynical catalyst Kenneth Richmond.

The first meaning of educational technology refers to the application of physical-science and engineering technology to provide mechanical or electro-mechanical tools, instrumentation, or 'hardware' which can be used for educational purposes. This is the principal sense in which the term has been used by Finn and other spokesmen for the 'audiovisual education' and by the electronic communications industry. In this sense, the reference is generally the use of equipment for presenting instructional materials, such as still and motion picture projectors (silent and sound), tape recorders (including the special arrangements employed as a 'language laboratory') television, 'teaching machines', and, most recently, computer-based training systems.

In the second sense, educational technology does not concern hardware, as such, but refers rather to a 'technology' in a generic sense, as a derivative or application of an underlying science —

somewhat as the technology of engineering relates to the science of physics or the technology of medical practice to the underlying biological sciences.

These two basic kinds of educational technology can interact in the design and use of instrumentation to provide better control over the learning situation, by providing a richer array of stimulus material (for example, through motion pictures), and also by providing for interaction between the responses of the learner and the presentation of instructional material.

Arthur Lumsdain, Educational Technology, Programmed Learning and Instructional Science in Hilgard, *Theories of Learning and Instruction*.

A useful distinction can be made between technology in education and technology of education. Technology in education refers to the increasingly complex range of audio-visual equipment now available in many schools and, in this sense, educational technology can explain to teachers the purposes and functions of different forms of equipment; provide training in the use of AV equipment to overcome the reluctance of teachers to use new media; and show the relevance of audio-visual equipment in the context of individualised learning as well as in more formal teacher/pupil relationships.

The strongest protagonists for educational technology are not, however, satisfied with a role limited to technology in education and the provision of audio-visual aids. They see themselves as crucially involved in the design and evaluation of systems of learning involving an understanding of the psychology of learning and of communication and information theory to be used to establish a rationale for good teaching practice which uses a variety of media and modes and which enables the teacher to deploy his skills more effectively and apply them more widely. This is the technology of education.

T.K. Robinson, Educational Technology and Curriculum Development. Scottish Education Department Inspectorate Bulletin 49. November 1976 (restricted circulation).

In my leisure time I happen to be a bird watcher. Because I use binoculars, telephoto lenses and computerised flash units — not to mention radar scanning for the study of migration — do I find it necessary to speak of ornithological technology? I do not. Why, then, as an educationist, should I indulge in loose, pretentious talk about educational technology?

W. Kenneth Richmond, *The Education Industry* (Methuen 1969).

If these views can be expressed about educational technology what can be said of the *educational technologist*? If there is a range of views that can be held with equal certainty about the true nature of educational technology then we are likely to find a range of people all carrying out different duties who either think of themselves, or are thought of, as educational technologists. A lighthearted, but penetrating view of the topic is taken by Dr Phillipe C. Duchastel in an article entitled 'On Being an Educational Technologist'.* Borrowing a model from Professor D.G. Hawkridge developed in 'Caricatures of Educational Evaluators' he portrays the educational technologist as:

Designer

He (merely a way of saying 'the person') is the creative artist, always looking about for new combinations of media, new teaching strategies. . . . He is often the good systems man as well, in that his designs are holistic and are usually seen to be efficient and effective.

Resource-person

When the course team doesn't quite know how to handle a particular aspect of the course, he comes forth with either a ready-made solution or alternatively a strategy for coming to grips with the situation.

Innovator

Here again his creative instincts are let loose within, but they now bear upon much more pervasive situations. He is after radical changes, no mere patch-up work.

Product quality verifier

The PQV tunes most of his energies towards checking that what goes out to students is presentable.

Editor

This one is the mad PQV whose style of commenting on drafts is indistinguishable from that of his colleague the editor.

Evaluator

He believes above all in feedback as the only way of improving the educational quality of uncertain materials during the first year of presentation. He has a twin, this one, the developmental tester.

* British Journal of Educational Technology, no. 3, vol. 9, October 1978.

Student

He has an assortment of wigs in his cupboard which he puts on in order to get the feel of 'now, how would this strike me if I were a way-below-average student?', etc.

Preacher

There are quite a few of these around. He has the word and his only frustration is when his course team colleagues won't listen to him; or worse yet when they do listen but fail to react.

Only competent educator

The former's cousin, embodied in the belief that academics don't care a damn about whether the students learn as long as the course (*a* course) goes out.

Diplomat

He is the politician whose greatest sin would be to arouse any suspicion at all about what he is about. He flows with the various tides that sweep through the course production process.

Problem-solver

Like the resource-person, he is problem-orientated but relies more on spontaneous ingenuity rather than on any set of procedures or prior experience.

Consolidator

He relies for his expertise on being able to disseminate time-and-tried ideas and strategies, building on the past rather than ever re-inventing.

Theoretician

He is quite above all the rest of this. His role in society is to redirect the paradigms of thought which encapsulate an issue at any given time. He likes to write.

Researcher I

The number-cruncher. Oh, what will he not do to put his hands on some down-to-earth numbers? He believes above all in reliability.

Researcher II

The field-researcher. He spends a good deal of his time with the natives (ie, the students) trying to find out what their customs are.

Certifier of quality education

He doesn't really have much to do except exist, and be pointed at. His mere presence represents educational quality.

Supporter of ideas

His forte is not so much in generating ideas as it is in backing up ideas of others which he considers worthy of his support.

Critic

His job is really to make sure that everyone sees the hidden implications of a given line of action. He likes to write long memos about these.

Reader

It is absolutely imperative that he give his hopefully esteemed opinion on each and every piece of material produced by the course team.

Dogsbody

He is usually given the task of writing assessment items, setting assessment parameters, etc.

Transformer

He takes rough drafts of units and spends most of his time polishing them up with all kinds of titbits.

Academic

He believes all members of the course team are educators as well as himself and offers his views as merely those of a colleague academic. A bit of pepper on the soup!

INDEX

acceptance of services 126
access to media 78-88
administration, responsibilities 138
affective change 36
amortisation periods 49
Anglo-American Cataloguing Rules 78
assessment procedures, need for 33
assimilation 130-2
audio copying 120
audio recording 113
audio-visual aids 35; department 15; equipment, installation 93; in colleges 21

best buy, hardware 49
Brynmor Jones Report 25
BUFC 67

catalogue, as a teaching tool 45
cataloguing 42; common system for books and non-books 44; methods 46; pro-forma 52; rate of input 50; software method 51; style of entry 44
CELPIS 67
centralisation of equipment 101; hardware 57; information 51, 53; software 74
centralised collection 77; control, maintenance 96-7; library 77; organisation 37
CET (UK) 67
change agent 13, 29
choice of resources 47
collation of resources 34
colleges, audio-visual units in 21; education 20-2; further education 15-20; higher education 22-5
combined catalogue, advantages 45
consultation, on media production 124
contacts catalogue 68-71
control of production 109
copying 110
costing decisions 112
creation of resources 34
criteria for organisation pattern 130
criteria for production 111; media centre 104

decentralised organisation 37
decision making 36; printing, equipment 115-20
departmental information 39; libraries 51, 76; resources 39
Development of Resource Centre 102
Dewey 43
dispersed collections 75
dissemination 132-4
distribution, hardware 57
Dundee College of Education 22, 73

educational development 127, 140; unit 15
educational technology, definitions of 11; as a spectrum 12
educational technology unit, services supplied by 28; function of 28-35, 42, 47; polytechnics 23; staffing 18-19; tasks associated with, distribution of 18-19
educational technologist: linker 29; manager 29; mediator 29; relations with other staff 28
equipment, algorithm 120; central bank 97; consultation 96; delivery system 101; for libraries 78-88, 89; installation 95-6; mobile 97; operators 93-4; safety 95; selection 91-2
evaluation procedures, need for 33
evaluation, software 64- 5; software, pro-forma 66
existing material 33-4; collation of 34
existing resources, collation of 34

film production 113-14

graphics 112
graphics artist 109

hardware 35; 'best buy' 49; catalogue, SCET, NCAVAE 48; centralisation 57; control of 37; distribution 57; information 54; inventory 55-6; location 56; maintenance 57, 60; mistakes 90, 92; new developments 48-9; ownership 57; planning for use 56

hardware purchase, information on 47; policy 48
hardware, sharing 68; under-use of 54, 55, 58, 59, 60
HELPIS 67

information 35, 36; centralisation 51, 53; control 39; software 50; hired software 63; incoming materials 62; inter-institution 67; hardware 54; network 68-71; system 37
inventory, hardware 55-6
installation of audio-visual equipment 93
installation of equipment 95-6
institutional setting 15-27
inter-institutional information 67

job descriptions 18-19

knowledge broker 29

LANCET cataloguing rules 78
liaison with staff 98
librarian 41, 42, 45, 46, 47; co-operation 51; co-operation with 36
library, centralised 77; departmental 51; equipment 89; hardware 78-88; role 88
listening 30
location of hardware 56

maintenance, central control 96; hardware 57, 60; mobile equipment 97, 98; organisation 96
media centre 102; model 104-6; other failures 108
media, decisions 36
media production, as staff development 124
media storage 77, 78, 88
methodology, influence of information 40
mobile equipment 97; maintenance 97-8

National Audio-Visual Aids Centre, hardware catalogue 48
non-book media, cataloguing 42
non-commercial resources 63

organisation, of maintenance 96; of software 74; of staff 135-9; of support services

packaging 120
photographics 113
planning, media centre 108-9
polytechnics 22-5; assimilation of educational technology 24; educational technology units 23
print, planning 115
production, consultation 124
production, control 109
production criteria 111
production function 110

questioning, techniques of 31-2

relationships with staff 56, 60, 62
repair service 99
reproduction 114
Resource Centre 102
resource centres, other failures 108
resource organisation 102
resources, choice of 47; non-commercial 63
role of library 88; production agency 124

safety of equipment 95
Scottish Council for Educational Technology: hardware catalogue 48; resource liaison project 54
selection of equipment 91-2
service modes 100; role 126
servicing equipment 96
services 107
software 35; acquisitions list 62; cataloguing method 51-2; centralisation 74; decisions on 36; dispersed 75; evaluation 64-5; evaluation, proforma 66; hired or borrowed 63; information 50; information accessibility 50; organisation 74
split sites 76
staff 135-9; development 127; development, through production 124; graphics 112; liaison 98; management 137; relationships 56, 60, 62; roles 136-7; status 136, 138, 139
status of staff 136, 138, 139
strategies for acceptance of services 126; assimilation 128, 130-2; dissemination 128, 132, 134; staff development 141
subject knowledge 31-4
support for library staff 89; services 15; services, organisation 73; systems 13

teachers, professional development of 21
teaching 16
technology in education 11-14
technology of education 11-14
threat of development 141
training 16
type-setting 113

underware 35
Unesco report 103
universal decimal classification 44
universities 25-7; staff training 26

video production 113; reproduction 120
vocational courses 15; education 15